A Guide to Hart-Parr, Oliver, and White Farm Tractors 1901-1996

Larry Gay

Published by the
American Society of Agricultural Engineers
2950 Niles Road, St. Joseph, Michigan

About ASAE — the Society for engineering in agricultural, food, and biological systems

ASAE is a technical and professional organization of members committed to improving agriculture through engineering. Many of our 8,000 members in the United Stated, Canada, and more than 100 other countries are engineering professionals actively involved in designing the farm equipment that continues to help the world's farmers feed the growing population. We're proud of the triumphs of the agriculture and equipment industry. ASAE is dedicated to preserving the record of this progress for others. This book joins many other popular ASAE titles in recording the exciting developments in agricultural equipment history.

A Guide to Hart-Parr, Oliver, and White Tractors, 1901-1996
Editor and Book Designer: Melissa Carpenter Miller

Library of Congress Catalog Card Number (LCCN) 97-75107
International Standard Book Number (ISBN) 0-929355-87-3

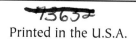

Printed in the U.S.A.

Acknowledgments

Sincere appreciation must be given to Mary Ann Townsend at the Floyd County Museum in Charles City, Iowa, who guided me through the museum's numerous files of information and photographs. Her efforts along with those of Frank and Jane McKinney made every trip to the museum a pleasure. Thanks to Sherry Schaefer for sharing her recently acquired collection of Hart-Parr and Oliver information and photographs. Her files provided some of the missing pieces of the puzzle and made this book more complete. Also a thank you to Les Stegh and Vicki Eller at the Deere & Company Archives for the use of their fine collection of trade magazines which supplied additional information.

The photographs of the experimental Oliver Chilled Plow Works tractor were provided by the Northern Indiana Historical Society and the Studebaker National Museum through the combined efforts of Robert and Jean Denham and Mary Renshaw.

A special note of appreciation goes to Bill Meeker, Sherry Schaefer, and Doug Strawser for reviewing the manuscript and offering suggestions, additional information, and some questions which required another round of research.

Thanks also to Blane Bolte, Lyle Spitznoggle, Todd Stockwell, John Schwiebert, Dean Tjaden, Wayne Wiltse, Keith Woods, and Landis Zimmerman for sharing their catalogs or contributing a special piece of information. And one more thank you to all the members of the Hart-Parr/Oliver Collectors Association who patiently answered all my questions about their tractors during the last three years.

And finally a special thank you to Donna Hull and Melissa Miller at ASAE for using their talents to create another fine book from an assortment of short articles and a series of photographs.

Dedication

This book is dedicated to Doug Strawser, a collector of Hart-Parr and Oliver tractors and a recognized historian of the companies and their products. Doug is a "walking encyclopedia" of information and served as my inspiration and mentor as I prepared this book.

About the Author

Larry Gay converted his boyhood fascination of farm machinery into a degree in Agricultural Engineering and then a 35-year career with Deere & Company. After retiring as the Manager of Engineering for the John Deere Merchandise Division, he wrote the book *Farm Tractors 1975-1995*. He became interested in Hart-Parr and Oliver tractors when he discovered Doug Strawser's experimental Oliver Chilled Plow tractor at an antique tractor show. The resulting search for information has resulted in a "Historical Highlights" page in each issue of the *Hart-Parr/Oliver Collector* magazine and this book.

Larry and his wife, Margie, live on a small acreage near Geneseo, Illinois, where a horse named Hank and an Oliver Super 55 tractor work together to keep the pasture mowed.

Table of Contents

Higher Horsepower with the Oliver Models

White — A New Name, Colors, and Styling

The AGCO White Models

Appendix

The Early Hart-Parr Tractors

C.W. HART

(1872-1937)

(1868-1941)

C.H. PARR

Hart-Parr No. 1 & No. 2
1901-1902

Charles W. Hart and Charles H. Parr received their mechanical engineering degrees from the University of Wisconsin on June 24, 1896, with special honors for their thesis about "An Investigation of Internal Combustion Engines." After graduation they built a 2-story, 31- x 56-foot building in Madison, Wisconsin, and started manufacturing stationary gasoline engines. As their engine business grew, they decided to add a second building in April 1900. Soon they needed to expand again, but land was expensive and Madison did not encourage industrial development. So they turned to Hart's hometown of Charles City, Iowa, where arrangements for a new factory were made. Construction started on July 5, 1901, and the relocation of the Madison operation was completed on December 25, 1901.

About this same time, Hart and Parr built their first gasoline traction engine by mounting one of their 30-horsepower stationary engines on a pipe frame chassis with steam engine wheels. Historians have not been consistent about when this occurred and even Hart and Parr may have had difficulty defining the day they "built" this experimental gasoline traction engine. Some of the Hart-Parr and early Oliver publications used the phrase "Built in 1901 and sold in 1902" to describe the event. However, it appears No. 1 was built, and undoubtedly rebuilt, during the winter of 1901-1902, and a better phrase may be "Started in 1901 and completed in 1902." The serial number of this machine, which would have been the engine serial number, is not known.

We do know that No. 1 was sold in mid-July 1902 to David Jennings of Clear Lake, Iowa, because the Charles City newspaper reported it broke through a bridge while it was being driven across country to its new owner. It remained in service for many years before becoming part of a scrap drive during World War I.

Hart-Parr No. 1 was built with a heavy transmission, so it was suitable for both drawbar and belt work. It was rated as a 17-30 tractor, developing 17 horsepower when used for drawbar work and 30 horsepower on the belt. The difference in the two numbers was due to the power loss in the

Hart-Parr No. 1 was built with a Hart-Parr 2-cylinder engine rated at 30 horsepower. The new Charles City office building is in the background.

transmission, the power required to propel the tractor, and the power loss due to slippage between the drive wheels and the ground.

The two-cylinder horizontal engine was built around a 9-inch bore and a 13-inch stroke and had a rated speed of 250 rpm. The crankshaft was located crosswise of the chassis, so the power could be transmitted to the rear wheels with a chain drive and spur gears. The engine was cooled with oil and in turn a bank of commercial cast-iron radiators and six expansion bulbs cooled the oil. The operator's platform was located at the rear of the tractor, behind the radiators.

Hart-Parr No. 2, again with a 17-30 rating, was assembled during the summer of 1902 and used the same size engine as No. 1, but with the engine cylinders inverted so the exhaust system pointed downward. No. 2 featured a new I-beam frame and an enclosed cylindrical shaped radiator, located at the front of the machine, which used an upward flow of air through the radiator for cooling. The transmission system was revised to include a bevel gear differential and a planetary clutch unit built into the belt pulley.

Hart-Parr No. 2 was sold to P. Wendeloe of South Dakota on July 15, 1903. The final fate of No. 2 is not known and a record of its serial number has not been found.

Hart-Parr No. 2 was pictured in the first advertisement for a gasoline traction engine in December 1902.

Hart-Parr No. 3 & Hart-Parr 17-30
1903-1906

Hart-Parr No. 3 differed from No. 1 and No. 2 in that it was not just one tractor, but one of a production run of 13 tractors built during the winter of 1902-1903. These tractors are considered the industry's first commercially successful production run of gasoline traction engines and is the basis for Hart-Parr being recognized as the "Founders of the Tractor Industry." The tractor from this first production run with serial number 1207 is the oldest surviving Hart-Parr and is the one known as Hart-Parr No. 3. However, it appears it was not the third one built, but it may have been the third one sold. Also an additional 17-30 model was built in 1903 with a slightly different type of engine construction, so there were 14 units of this size produced for the year.

These No. 3 type of tractors were classified as 17-30 tractors and continued to use the 2-cylinder engine with the 9-inch bore and 13-inch stroke. The 4-cycle gasoline engine was positioned horizontally with the crankshaft crosswise of the tractor and with the cylinder heads toward the rear of the tractor. The globe-shaped cylinder heads were cast as part of the cylinder, thus eliminating the need for gaskets, which were unreliable at that time.

This engine was the valve-in-head type with the intake valves opened by suction and closed with a spring. Push rods were used to open and close the exhaust valves on all the 17-30 tractors and once again the

After "Old Hart-Parr No. 3" was repurchased, the original canopy was replaced with one which advertised it as the oldest gasoline tractor in the world.

exhaust system was pointed upward with the vertical exhaust pipes passing through the canopy over the engine. The engine was oil cooled with the oil being circulated through the cylindrical radiator at the front of the machine with the relief exhaust helping induce an upward air flow through the radiator.

The engine speed was limited to 270 rpm with a hit-and-miss type of governor. The I-beam frame and the planetary clutch in the belt pulley were retained from No. 2 as was the bevel gear differential which was built for threshing operations.

The Shop Order card for Serial Number 1207 was completed by Parr who described it as a 17-horsepower traction engine. It was sold on August 5, 1903, for $1,580 to George Mitchell who farmed south of Charles City. In December 1903 one of the first field improvement programs took place when the company sent Mitchell six improved items such as ignitor springs and push rod levers. Then in May 1905 the company replaced the cylindrical radiator with the more efficient, square-shaped radiator which had been "put out on quite a number of engines" in 1904.

In 1924 the company repurchased the tractor from Mitchell and exhibited it at state fairs and other events. From 1932 to 1948 it was at the Museum of Science and Industry in Chicago and then it moved to Battle Creek, Michigan, for the Oliver Centennial celebration on June 30, 1948. Since then it has become part of the Smithsonian collection and has been exhibited at the Smithsonian and other museums. Currently it is on exhibit at a museum in Kirtland, Ohio.

Over the years Hart-Parr checked on the usage of what they referred to as their first 15 tractors and used this information in their advertising. In 1925 the company proudly advertised that 7 of these 15 tractors were still giving service. Six of the 15 were still in operation in 1928.

One of the first 17-30 models with the round radiator, the fuel tank under the engine, and the vertical exhaust stacks. The belt idler beside the radiator was not a part of the tractor.

Hart-Parr 22-40 &
Hart-Parr 22-45
1903-1907 & 1908-1911

The Hart-Parr Company also built 24 units of the model 22-40 in 1903. The 22-40 used the largest size of stationary engine which Hart-Parr had been building, a 40-horsepower, 2-cylinder horizontal engine with a 10-inch bore and a 15-inch stroke. This engine resulted in an enormous displacement of 2,356 cubic inches. The cylinder heads were again located toward the rear of the tractor and the exhaust system was pointed upward.

Although most historical books about tractors do not include the Hart-Parr 22-40 model, the Hart-Parr sales catalogs issued from 1904 through 1907 described the tractor with the 10- x 15-inch bore and stroke as a 22-40. During 1908 the compression ratio was increased and the 1908 through 1911 sales catalogs identified the tractor as a 22-45. This rerating process eventually caused many of the later company publications to refer to all of these tractors as the 22-45 model.

Although No. 2 was a radial departure from No. 1, the changes after No. 2 were ones of refinement. For example, the 22-40 model was developed for heavy traction work and three of the units built in 1903 were equipped with an experimental differential which used spur gears instead of bevel gears. This stronger and heavier "plow gear" enabled the tractor to be used for heavy tillage work and was used on most of the 22-40 models built in 1904 and 1905. It was used on all the 22-40s built in 1906. These plowing engines were the first ones with both the exhaust and the relief exhaust routed to the radiator to improve the draft up through the radiator. Also, the radiator was revised and the square type with the exposed radiator sections replaced the enclosed cylindrical type.

Some problems were experienced in the field with the operation of the valves, and as a result a new system with overhead cams was designed. Known as the rotary valve, this system is easily identified by the line shaft positioned along the left side of the engine. Starting in 1906 all 22-40 tractors were equipped with the rotary valve system.

This 1907 advertisement illustrated the 22-40 model with the rear-mounted tank for the gravity fuel system and the rerouted exhaust system to the top of the square type of radiator.

During 1905 the fuel tank mounted under the tractor and the required fuel pump were replaced with a gravity feed system. Also in 1905 the availability of gasoline began to decline and the price became more expensive. As a result Hart and Parr developed a carburetor during the winter of 1905-1906 which permitted their engines to burn kerosene. The carburetor was actually a double unit which also added water to prevent preignition of the kerosene and became a standard feature on the units built in 1906. A force-feed lubricator replaced the old sight glass system in 1907.

As the sales of gasoline traction engines continued to grow, it was decided to discontinue the line of stationary engines in 1905. Thus the Hart-Parr Company became the first company devoted exclusively to the production of gasoline/kerosene traction engines. In 1907 W. H. Williams, Hart-Parr's sales manager, started using the word "tractor" to replace "gasoline traction engine" in their advertisements. As a result, Hart-Parr is recognized as making "tractor" a universally accepted word, although it was later discovered the word had been used in an 1890 patent.

Almost all of the 22-45 tractors were equipped with the heavier differential with the spur gears which resulted in them being classified as a "plowing engine."

The 1912 Hart-Parr sales catalog rated this Hart-Parr tractor as a 30-60. Due to its dependability, it was also known as "Old Reliable."

Hart-Parr 30-60, Old Reliable
1911-1916

Again with the 30-60 we have the same confusion concerning when the first units were built. Traditional records and listings state the 30-60 models started in 1907, but the Hart-Parr sales catalogs of 1908 through 1911 described this tractor as a 22-45 with an engine which could develop 60 horsepower for a short time. Since there was not much difference between the two models Hart-Parr advertised as a 22-45 and the rerated 30-60, it appears all of these tractors eventually were described as a 30-60 model.

A 1912 catalog stated the 30-60 tractors were built with the 2-cylinder horizontal engine with the 10-inch bore, the 15-inch stroke, and the rotary valve system (cam shaft) which operated the valves. Engine speed was 300 rpm. The carburetor was built to handle kerosene and water, so there were three tanks on the tractor — a large one for kerosene, a small one for the gasoline required to start the engine, and one for water located above the engine. The engine was also equipped with a magneto and a force-feed lubricator. All the 30-60 units were oil cooled and used the square type radiator.

The drive train consisted of massive spur gears, all exposed, and the stronger differential built with spur gears. The rear axle had been increased to 5 inches in diameter and the rear wheels with a "wave" type of lug were 66 inches in diameter and 24 inches wide. The parts catalog suggested the 5-inch axle as the replacement for a worn or broken 4-inch axle, so many of the earlier tractors were upgraded. The only speed was 2.3 mph in forward and reverse.

The operator's platform remained at the rear where the steering wheel and control lever were located on the right side. The right rear wheel was partially covered with a short fender which provided some protection for the operator from dust and dirt. An overhead canopy extended from the rear of the tractor to about the front of the engine. The tractor continued to be steered by rotating the entire front axle by means of chains which were wound and released by a drum under the tractor.

The rotary valve system used a line shaft along the left side of the engine and a set of bevel gears to power the cam shaft which opened and closed the engine valves.

The new owner of Serial Number 4214 received a copy of this performance chart which showed it produced over 60 horsepower for 10.5 hours during its "run-in" on December 9, 1911.

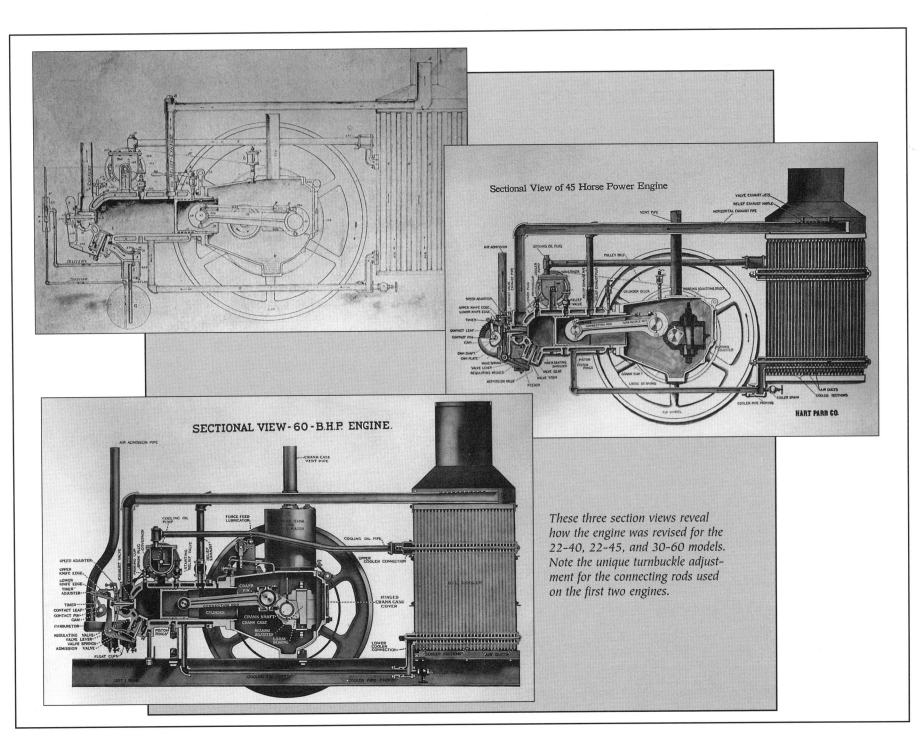

Sectional View of 45 Horse Power Engine

VALVE EXHAUST JETS
RELIEF EXHAUST NIPPLE
HORIZONTAL EXHAUST PIPE

VENT PIPE

AIR ADMISSION
COOLING OIL PLUG
PULLEY BELT
GOVERNOR
CYLINDER OILER
BEARING ADJUSTING STUDS

SPEED ADJUSTER
UPPER KNIFE EDGE
LOWER KNIFE EDGE
TIMER
CONNECTING ROD
TURN BUCKLE ROD
SPRING ADJUSTER

CONTACT LEAF
CONTACT PIN
CAM
PISTON
PISTON RINGS

CAM SHAFT
CAM PLATE
VALVE SPRING
VALVE LEVER
REGULATING VALVES
ADMISSION VALVE
FEEDER
INNER BEARING SHOULDER
VALVE SEAT
VALVE STEM
CRANK SHAFT
LOOSE BEARING

FLY WHEEL
COOLER PIPE PACKING
COOLER DRAIN
AIR DUCTS
COOLER SECTIONS

HART PARR CO.

SECTIONAL VIEW - 60 - B.H.P. ENGINE.

AIR ADMISSION PIPE
CRANK CASE VENT PIPE
COOLING OIL PUMP
FORCE FEED LUBRICATOR
OIL TANK FOR OIL WATER
COOLING OIL PIPE
UPPER COOLER CONNECTION

SPEED ADJUSTER
UPPER KNIFE EDGE
LOWER KNIFE EDGE
TIMER
TIMER ADJUSTER
STARTING RELIEF VALVE
PRIMING CUP
SPARK PLUG
GOVERNOR
CONTACT LEAF
CONTACT PIN
CAM
CARBURETOR
REGULATING VALVE
VALVE LEVER
VALVE SPRINGS
ADMISSION VALVE
FLOAT CUPS
PISTON RINGS
CYLINDER
PISTON
CONNECTING ROD
CRANK PIN
CRANK SHAFT
CRANK CASE
BEARING ADJUSTER
LOOSE BEARING
HINGED CRANK CASE COVER
OIL COOLER

EXHAUST BOX
RELIEF EXHAUST

LEFT I BEAM
COOLING TUBE SYSTEM
COOLER PIPE PACKING
LOWER COOLER CONNECTION
COOLER SECTIONS
AIR DUCTS

These three section views reveal how the engine was revised for the 22-40, 22-45, and 30-60 models. Note the unique turnbuckle adjustment for the connecting rods used on the first two engines.

The 40-80 represented new ideas with its opposed 4-cylinder engine, two closely spaced front wheels, the operator's station above the engine, and the radiators at the back.

Hart-Parr 40-80
1908-1909

The growing popularity of the Hart-Parr tractor soon resulted in the existing Charles City factory being used to capacity. In April 1905 the company decided to extend the 80- x 210-foot machine shop building by 314 feet. Late in 1906 plans were made for a new 100- x 600-foot erecting shop. When this building was completed, the Hart-Parr Company had enough space to build a second tractor model without compromising the production of the 22-45 model, so they developed the 40-80 with 80 belt horsepower and introduced it at the 1908 Minnesota State Fair.

However, this huge tractor was too large for one unskilled person to operate and thus it didn't appeal to many potential customers. Only ten model 40-80 tractors were built: four in 1908 and six in 1909.

The power plant was a horizontal 4-cylinder engine which the 1911 sales catalog rated at 110 maximum engine horsepower. The cylinders, with a 9- x 13-inch bore and stroke, were arranged in an opposed pattern with two on each side of the cross-mounted crankshaft. Two radiators were used, one for each half of the engine. The tanks for the kerosene, gasoline, and water were mounted in a horizontal position at the back of the tractor.

The tractor was equipped with 98-inch diameter x 28-inch wide rear drive wheels. The front wheels were spaced relatively close together. The operator's platform was located above the engine, so high above the ground that a ladder was provided for the operator. The view to the front would have been great from this lofty perch and the view to the rear wasn't as poor as it appears because the platform was offset to the right and the radiators to the left. The total weight of this tractor was about 34,000 pounds.

Hart-Parr 60-100
About 1911 or 1912

The huge 60-100 model was powered by a 4-cylinder vertical engine with the crankshaft in line with the chassis, the first Hart-Parr tractor with this configuration.

The 40-80 was not the largest tractor built by the Hart-Parr Company. Photographs were taken of a 60-100 model and the one in the photographs may have been the only example built. There is some thought that it was built for a special application, because the small sales of the 40-80 did not justify trying to market an even larger agricultural model.

This giant tractor was powered with a 4-cylinder, vertical type of engine in which the crankshaft was positioned lengthwise with the tractor. This in turn would require a different type of transmission and final drive as compared to the other Hart-Parr models. The engine was located toward the right side of the tractor and the two square type radiators were located toward the left side

The 60-100 model was not included in any of the Hart-Parr sales catalogs. Also the 60-100 is not listed in the company serial number and production records, but there are two missing serial numbers in 1912. Therefore, if one or two were built, they probably were considered to be experimental tractors.

The 60-100 was operated with a series of disk plows providing the load. With this model the ladder to the operator's station was at the back of the tractor.

Hart-Parr 15-30
1909-1911

Next the Hart-Parr Company turned its attention to smaller tractors for the Midwest farms where fences enclosed the fields. The fences required the tractors to be able to turn in tighter spaces. The first attempt in 1909 was the 15-30 model with a horizontal engine and a single front wheel. The power plant was a 2-cylinder engine with a 8- x 9-inch bore and stroke. Seven of these models were built, but they were not successful and all were recalled by the company.

The second attempt in 1910 was more successful as the horizontal engine was replaced with a vertical type. The vertical Hart-Parr engine resulted in a more compact design with the square radiator positioned just ahead of the engine and the single front wheel placed ahead of the radiator.

The new 2-cylinder vertical engine had the same 8-inch bore as the horizontal one, but the stroke was increased to 12 inches. Also the rated speed was reduced from 500 rpm to 400 rpm. The speed of the engine was now controlled with a throttle system using a centrifugal ball governor and could be adjusted on-the-go from 300 rpm to 450 rpm. This tractor was equipped with a 50-gallon kerosene tank, a 27-gallon water tank, and a 6-gallon gasoline tank.

The variety of crops grown in the Midwest meant the tractors had to be versatile, so the 15-30 was equipped with a 2-speed transmission in which a hand lever was used to position a sliding pair of pinion gears. Now the operator had a choice of 2.2 mph for heavy drawbar loads or 4.0 mph for lighter loads. To compensate for this faster "road speed," springs were built into the front wheel mounting and at the rear of the tractor. The reverse speed was still provided by the planetary clutch in the belt pulley. One of the 15-30 models has been restored by a collector in North Dakota.

This photo illustrates the configuration of both the vertical engine version of the 15-30 and the 20-40 with its vertical engine.

Hart-Parr 20-40
1911-1914

The 20-40 with some minor improvements replaced the 15-30, but without any major changes in the configuration. Again a rerating took place as the 20-40 was rated at ten more belt horsepower with the same basic 2-cylinder, 8- x 12-inch bore and stroke vertical engine.

The Hart-Parr engine for the 15-30 and the 20-40 was unique with the centerline of the crankshaft offset 2.75 inches from the center of the piston and a special shape for the connecting rods to prevent them from hitting the cylinder walls. Lubrication of the major parts of the 20-40 engine was accomplished with pressure from the engine explosions being piped to the crankcase which caused oil to splash into shallow pans from which the revolving connecting rods scooped oil. Special shelves on the sides of the crankcase caught some of the splashed oil and carried it to the main bearings.

With the type of power train used on the 15-30 and 20-40, there were only two shafts between the engine and the rear axle, the cross shaft with the sliding gear with two sizes of pinions and the differential shaft which in turn drove the rear wheels.

The rear wheels, with the wave type of lugs, were 73 inches in diameter and 20 inches wide. An internal type of spur gear was attached to the inside of the rim of the rear wheel and was driven by the master pinion gear. The front wheel for the 20-40 was slightly smaller in diameter at 48 inches, but 50 percent wider with a width of 18 inches. The Floyd County Historical Society now owns the only known restored Hart-Parr 20-40.

The product life cycle of the Hart-Parr 15-30 with the horizontal engine was rather short with seven being produced and seven being recalled.

Hart-Parr 12-27 & Hart-Parr 18-35
1913-1914 & 1914-1919

Right Side "35"

This 18-35 can be identified by the routing of the exhaust to the side of the radiator, instead of to the front as did the 12-27.

The next smaller tractor model built by the Hart-Parr Company was the 12-27 which retained the tricycle type of configuration and the vertical type of engine used by the 20-40. However, it was different in that the front wheel was actually two wheels which were closely spaced, this Hart-Parr engine had only one cylinder instead of two, and the radiator was located behind the engine instead of in front of it. The 12-27 started with a horizontal frame behind the front wheels and with the fuel and water tanks on the outside of the canopy, but soon changed to a curved front frame and relocated the fuel and water tanks under the canopy.

The vertical engine cylinder had an 8.50-inch bore, a 10-inch stroke, and a rated speed of 500 rpm. Although the engine could burn a variety of liquid fuels, it was designed to burn kerosene and was equipped with a water feed to prevent preignition under a heavy load. The exhaust was directed to the front of the oil-filled radiator to induce an upward air flow. The radiator was located directly in front of the operator's station and although it was not as wide as it was long, it somewhat limited the operator's forward view. The engine was lubricated with a force-feed oiler.

After building 224 of the 12-27 model, Hart-Parr redirected the exhaust to the right side of the radiator and enlarged the engine to a 10-inch bore which upgraded the rating to 18-35. It was advertised as being able to pull five or six 14-inch plow bottoms and thus plow 15 to 18 acres in a 10-hour day. The 18-35 was the only model Hart-Parr entered at

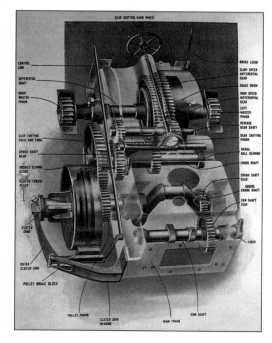

This phantom view shows how one steel casting served as the engine crankcase, the transmission case, and the tractor's frame. The hand wheel was used to shift gears.

the Fremont, Nebraska, Tractor Trials in August 1914. This tractor was also known as the Oil King 35 and it proved to be a popular model, remaining in production through 1919.

The 18-35 contained only 300 manufactured parts, 500 to 1,200 fewer than other makes. For example, one steel casting was used as the frame, the engine crankcase, and the transmission case. Since the crankshaft was positioned across the tractor, this one casting supported the cam shaft, crankshaft, the transmission cross shaft, the reverse gear shaft, and the differential shaft with a pinion gear on each end which in turn engaged the internal spur gear in each of the rear wheels. The cast-steel rear wheels had the wave form of lug, but an angle type of cleat could be added for additional traction.

The transmission provided two forward speeds of 1.8 and 2.6 mph and a reverse gear. Changing gears was accomplished with a hand wheel which operated a rack-and-pinion type of shifting mechanism. The engine speed was adjusted with a hand lever which changed the tension of a spring in the governor. The 18-35 even provided a spring seat for the comfort of the operator.

The 18-35 was equipped with a 30-gallon tank for kerosene which used a gravity feed because it was mounted in the top of the canopy. The main 20-gallon water tank was mounted above the engine and its water was used to mix with the kerosene and to cool just the cylinder head of the engine. In turn this kept the water warm enough to prevent freezing in cold weather. An auxiliary 30-gallon water tank was also mounted in the top of the canopy. Such a small amount of gasoline was needed for starting that a gasoline tank was not provided.

Hart-Parr Little Devil
1914-1916

The star attraction at the 1913 and 1914 Tractor Trials in Fremont, Nebraska, was the small, lightweight Bull tractor with three wheels, but with only one drive wheel. It pulled a 2-bottom plow and appealed to the smaller, general farmer. As a result Hart-Parr quickly developed a unique, three-wheeled tractor for the Midwest farmer. Instead of having a model number, it was named the Little Devil and was painted red.

Rated as a 15-22 tractor with a weight of 6,600 pounds, the Little Devil had a front axle with enough width and clearance to straddle two rows of corn. The front axle was attached rigidly to the frame and the single 64-inch diameter drive wheel was located at the rear of the tractor, on the centerline of the tractor in order to fit between the two rows of corn. The upholstered operator's seat and steering wheel were located on the right side of the tractor, beside the shielded rear drive wheel. Front wheel steering was the "automotive" type.

In order to reduce the cost and weight of this tractor, it was designed to be as simple as possible and used a minimum of parts. The engine was a two-cycle Hart-Parr engine with two horizontal cylinders. Thus the valves used in a regular Hart-Parr four-cycle engine and their related cams, springs, and drive train parts were replaced with two ports in the wall of each cylinder which were uncovered as the 5.50-inch diameter piston moved toward the crankshaft, near the end of its 7-inch stroke. The engine was positioned with the crankshaft crosswise of the tractor with a flywheel on the left end and the belt pulley on the right end. The operating engine speed was listed as 600 rpm, with an operating range of 500 to 750 rpm. The engine started on gasoline, ran on kerosene, and an early type of fuel injection system eliminated the carburetor.

The drive train was built as simple as possible with only seven gears used to reduce the engine speed to the drive wheel speed. The first gear was the pinion on the crankshaft and the seventh was the internal spur gear built into the rear wheel. The first five gears were in a gearcase and ran in oil. A lever permitted the driver to select forward or reverse by rotating the front of the gearcase up or down. For example, the tractor could be shifted from the forward speed of 3.3 mph to the reverse speed of 2.2 mph.

The Little Devil represented simplicity with its two-cycle engine and the front of the gearcase behind the belt pulley moving up or down to shift gears.

The unique feature of the Little Devil was the capability to reverse the rotation of the two-cycle engine. This then provided the operator with a forward speed of 2.2 mph and a reverse speed of 3.3 mph. And thus a tractor with only seven gears in its drive train provided two forward speeds and two in reverse.

A total of 725 Little Devil tractors were built — 26 in 1914, 499 in 1915, and 200 in 1916. However, the Little Devil had two problems. The tractor had a tendency to tip toward the right, so a skid was added under the operator's station to limit the tilt angle. But the more serious problem concerned the propensity of the engine, as it lugged down under a heavy load, to suddenly reverse itself and thus the direction of travel of the tractor. As a result the Hart-Parr Company recalled the tractors and destroyed them. By the end of 1918 General Manager W. R. Dray reported, "The Little Devils have been bought back or traded in until they are largely forgotten." Only a few of the 725 tractors have survived and fewer operate, including one owned by the Floyd County Historical Society in Charles City and one by a collector in Kansas.

The flywheel side of the Little Devil included the fuel tank which was located in different positions on the frame and fender during its three years of production.

9

A New Design of Hart-Parr Tractors

New Hart-Parr (12-25) & Hart-Parr 30 (15-30 A)

1918-1922

The New Hart-Parr was introduced in 1918, after Charles Hart left the company in 1917, and was the first model of a new basic design which was built until mid-1930. It was originally rated as a 12-25 tractor, but after some minor improvements were made during the first year, the rating was changed to a 3-plow tractor with 30 belt horsepower and the tractor was reidentified as the model 30. After the Nebraska Tractor Tests were started in 1920, the "official" rating became 15-30.

This new Hart-Parr tractor was built around a cast-steel frame made in Hart-Parr's steel foundry. The 2-cylinder engine was positioned horizontally with the crankshaft crosswise of the tractor and the cylinder heads toward the rear of the tractor. The engine was positioned toward the right side of the tractor and the transmission was located on the left side. The engine was now cooled with water and the radiator fan blew air forward through the honeycomb-type radiator. The water pump was driven by the radiator fan shaft, which in turn was powered by a friction drive from the flywheel.

The Hart-Parr 2-cylinder valve-in-head engine had a 6.50- x 7.00-inch bore and stroke and a rated speed of 750 rpm. It was built to burn kerosene and was equipped with a Kerosene Shunt which fed cold fuel directly to the carburetor under full load, but passed it through a heating chamber in the exhaust manifold when the engine was under a light load.

The Madison-Kipp force-feed lubricator provided 30 drops of

The Hart-Parr 15-30 A had a lowered fuel tank, a drive shaft for the radiator fan, and the exhaust system routed through the front frame casting.

oil per minute to the pistons and 15 drops per minute to the connecting rod and crankshaft bearings when it was properly adjusted. The excess oil was collected in the crankcase and the overflow was used to wash and lubricate the open gears mounted in the rear drive wheels. The intake and exhaust valves were operated with exposed push rods and the exhaust was directed downward on the first of the New Hart-Parrs, but was directed forward under the radiator on the Hart-Parr 30.

The sliding spur gear transmission provided two forward speeds of 2 and 3 mph, "the proper speed for the best plowing and discing," plus a reverse speed of 1.5 mph. Next to the vertical gear shift lever was the vertical clutch lever which activated the band-type clutch located in the flywheel. The final drive was an internal gear bolted to the inside rim of the 52-inch diameter x 10-inch wide rear wheels.

The operator's platform was located at the rear of the tractor with the seat and steering wheel offset to the right side. The steering wheel transmitted the operator's efforts through a series of U-joints to a worm gear which operated a gear sector next to the right front wheel. The model 30 used the "automotive" type of steering for the front wheels.

The Hart-Parr 30 (15-30 A) was tested at the Nebraska Tractor Test Laboratory in June 1920. It was the 26th tractor tested by these new tests which would become the standard for the industry. The results of these tests were:

The first experimental version of the Hart-Parr 12-25 and 15-30 A used a belt drive for the radiator fan and water pump and had an exposed gear between the flywheel and belt pulley.

Model	Test No.	Type of Test	Drawbar Hp	Belt Hp
Hart-Parr 30 Kerosene	26	Rated	15.37	30.22
		Maximum	19.65	31.37

11

The Hart-Parr 10-20 B had its water pump located on the right end of the governor and the push rods and rocker arms were covered. Also the rear part of the fenders was shortened.

Hart-Parr 20 (10-20 B)
1920-1922

In 1920 Hart-Parr started manufacturing the model 20 which was a smaller version of the model 30. It was classified as a 2-plow tractor and was also known as the 10-20 B after its tests at Nebraska in 1921. The overall configuration of the 20 was very similar to the 30, but the dimensions and weight were less.

The 20 was powered with a Hart-Parr 2-cylinder engine which was mounted on a cast-steel frame. The engine speed of 800 rpm was slightly faster than the 30 and the bore and stroke were a smaller 5.25 x 6.50 inches. The 20 was equipped with the Kerosene Shunt and the Madison-Kipp lubricator. Refinements, compared to the 15-30 A, included relocating the water pump to the right end of the governor, covering the push rods and rocker arms, and moving the gear shift lever to the top of the transmission case.

The model 20 had two forward speeds of 2 and 3 mph plus one speed in reverse. It also used the same band type of clutch as the 30 and the same open type of final drive in the rear wheels. However, the rear wheels were smaller with a 46-inch diameter and a 10-inch width. The angle iron lugs were standard, but the 20 was tested at Nebraska with 3.5-inch high spade lugs.

The Hart-Parr 20 (10-20 B) was tested at Nebraska in June 1921. The test report noted the clutch grabbed, making smooth starting practically impossible, and listed the following results:

Model	Test No.	Type of Test	Drawbar Hp	Belt Hp
Hart-Parr 20 Kerosene	79	Rated	11.23	20.12
		Maximum	14.08	23.01

Hart-Parr 30 (15-30 C)
1922-1924

Right side view of Hart-Parr "30."

The long tapered frame can be quickly identified by noting the rear-mounting bracket for the fuel tank bolts to the top of the frame.

During 1922 the Hart-Parr 30 was revised and the model designation changed from 15-30 A to 15-30 C. The overall configuration remained the same and the model number on the side of the fuel tank continued to be 30.

The 15-30 A used a tapered cast-steel frame and two parallel channel members which extended forward. For the 15-30 C, the frame became two long channel members which extended from the rear axle to the front axle. These two channels were formed to provide the

Advertisements for the 15-30C emphasized its operator comfort with a large platform and easy-to-reach controls.

wide spacing at the rear and the narrow spacing at the front. Cross members were hot riveted to the channels to provide a base for the engine. Since the change in width of the frame now extended over a longer distance, the rear mounting bracket for the fuel tank was bolted to the top of the frame instead of the side.

The basic engine for the 15-30 C did not change with its 6.50-inch bore, 7.00-inch stroke, and 750-rpm engine speed. However, the push rods and rocker arms were now enclosed, the water pump was relocated to the governor frame, and the radiator now used copper tubes and fins in a cast-iron frame.

The gear shift mechanism was revised and the shift lever was relocated to the top of the transmission case. However, the two forward speeds remained at 2 and 3 mph and the final drive continued to be the open gears located on the inside rim of the rear wheels. The fenders were the shorter type, first introduced on the late 15-30 A tractors, in which the rear portion no longer extended down to the level of the operator's platform. The Hart-Parr 15-30 C was not tested at the Nebraska Tractor Testing Laboratory.

Cutout view, Hart-Parr "30." Simple to operate. Accessible for adjustments. Convenient for operator.

This top view of the 15-30 C model shows the new long tapered frame, the relocated water pump, the new type of gear shift lever, and the shorter operator's platform.

Hart-Parr 20 (10-20 C)
1922-1924

Also during 1922 the 10-20 B was revised and the model designation was changed to 10-20 C. The overall configuration remained the same and the model 20 designation on the side of the fuel tank was continued.

The cast-steel frame and its two parallel channel members which served as the basic structure for the 10-20 B were discontinued on the 10-20 C. The frame for the 10-20 C was two long channel members, with hot riveted cross members, which extended from the rear axle to the front axle. Today these full length channels are easy to identify with the change in the width of the frame extending over a long distance.

For the 10-20 C, the engine bore was increased from 5.25 to 5.50 inches. The 6.50 inch stroke did not change, so the engine displacement increased from 281 to 308 cubic inches. This should have resulted in a power increase, but the power rating remained at 10-20 and the tractor continued to be listed as a 2-plow tractor with an engine speed of 800 rpm. The radiator was revised to the type used on the 15-30 C with copper tubes in a cast-iron frame.

The published travel speeds increased from 2 and 3 mph to 2.3 and 3.3 mph. The reverse speed was now listed as 1.5 mph. Features that were continued from the 10-20 B included the contracting band type of clutch, the final drive with the open gears bolted to the inside rim of the rear wheels, and the short rear fenders.

The Hart-Parr 10-20 C was not tested at the Nebraska Tractor Testing Laboratory.

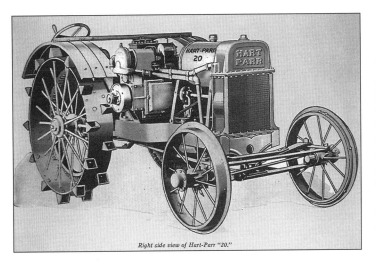

Right side view of Hart-Parr "20."

With the change to the long tapered channel frame, the rear support bracket for the fuel tank was bolted to the top of the frame. The size of the engine also changed for the 10-20 C model.

13

The configuration of the Hart-Parr 22-40 followed the other two models, but it was a much heavier tractor with a 4-cylinder engine built from two 10-20 C blocks.

Hart-Parr 40 (22-40)

1923-1927

A third model was added to the Hart-Parr line of tractors in 1923. The new model 40 was classified as a 4-plow tractor with a rating of 22 drawbar horsepower and 40 belt horsepower. Although the 40 was larger and weighed almost 2,000 pounds more than the 30, its overall configuration was similar to the 30. It too used the riveted type of frame with the full length channels.

The "Twin-Two" engine for the 40 was unique because it was basically two 10-20 C engines, again in a horizontal position with the cylinder heads toward the rear of the tractor and the crankshaft located crosswise of the tractor. There were two blocks with two cylinders in each block, but one crankcase. The bore and stroke of 5.50 x 6.50 inches matched the 20, so the displacement was 616 cubic inches, twice that of the the 20 . The rated engine speed was listed as 750 rpm in the tractor's manual, but it was 800 rpm at the Nebraska tests. The engine was lubricated with a Madison-Kipp lubricator and the water pump was driven from the governor shaft.

The 2-speed transmission of the 40 provided forward speeds of 2 and 3 mph which matched the 30. The contracting band type of clutch was used for the first two years and the plate clutch for the last three years. The

The operator and engine were positioned on the right side of the tractor with the flywheel, transmission, and belt pulley on the left side.

final drive was similar to the other two models with an internal spur gear bolted to the inside of each of the wider 13-inch rear wheels. The 14-inch diameter belt pulley provided the same belt speed as the Hart-Parr 30.

The Hart-Parr 40 was tested at Nebraska in July 1923 with the following results:

Model	Test No.	Type of Test	Drawbar Hp	Belt Hp
Hart-Parr 40 Kerosene	97	Rated	21.62	40.66
		Maximum	28.23	46.40

Hart-Parr 16-30 E & Hart-Parr 16-30 F
1924-1925 & 1926

The 16-30 E replaced the open spur gears on the inside rim of the rear wheels with an enclosed set of spur gears. It was also equipped with a new dry-plate clutch.

The 15-30 C was replaced with the 16-30 E model which indicates the drawbar horsepower was increased and other improvements were made. The overall configuration of the tractor and its engine remained unchanged. The differences between the 16-30 E and the 16-30 F were minor.

Two major improvements were made in the drive train. The contracting band clutch, which had been used since the New Hart-Parr model, was replaced with a dry-plate disc clutch. The clutch was still located on the flywheel.

Also the open, internal-type spur gears which were attached to the inside of the rims of the rear wheels were replaced with an enclosed set of spur gears. The new large external-type spur gears were attached to the rear wheel. These gears were in an oil-tight, dust-proof stamped steel enclosure on each side of the tractor which provided an oil bath for the gears.

Although the basic size of the engine was still the same as the Hart-Parr 30 (15-30 A) tested in 1920, the improved performance of the 16-30 E was demonstrated by its test at Nebraska in October 1924. For example, the fuel efficiency improved from 6.62 to 8.06 hp-hr/gal during the maximum belt power test. The power results were:

Model	Test No.	Type of Test	Drawbar Hp	Belt Hp
Hart-Parr 16-30 E Kerosene	106	Rated	16.79	30.33
		Maximum	24.79	37.03

The 12-24 E was revised to include a new steering system, a dry-plate clutch on the left side of the flywheel, and enclosed spur gears for the rear wheels as shown on this 12-24.

Hart-Parr 12-24 E
1924-1926

The 10-20 C was replaced in 1924 with the 12-24 E which was advertised as a 2-3 plow tractor. Although there was no change in the basic dimensions of the Hart-Parr engine, there was an increase of 20 percent in the rated drawbar and belt horsepowers. Actually, the power increase started with the 10-20 C when the bore size was enlarged, but the advertised power rating was not increased at that time. The remainder of the increase had to come from better efficiency and other improvements.

The 12-24 E kept pace with the 16-30 E by replacing its contracting band clutch with a dry-plate disc clutch. The 12-24 E also replaced the open final drive gears and the live rear axle with an enclosed set of spur gears on each side of the tractor. The rear wheels now rotated on a stationary rear axle.

New for both the 12-24 E and the 16-30 E was a new steering system in which an enclosed worm gear set at the lower end of the steering column replaced the open worm and gear sector on the front axle.

The 12-24 E was tested at Nebraska at the same time as the 16-30 E (October 1924). The rated drawbar test carried a note that the horsepower was below its rating because the operator did not apply enough load and that the tractor would have easily pulled its rating. The test results were:

Model	Test No.	Type of Test	Drawbar Hp	Belt Hp
Hart-Parr 12-24 E Kerosene	107	Rated	11.57	24.24
		Maximum	17.54	26.97

Hart-Parr 18-36 G & Hart-Parr 18-36 H & I
1926-1927 & 1927-1930

During this era Hart-Parr emphasized durability by citing examples of continuous running. In one case a farmer in Australia plowed non-stop with his Hart-Parr tractor for 11 days for a record of 264 hours.

The 2-cylinder Hart-Parr engine which had used a 6.50 x 7.00 inch bore and stroke since 1918 was revised to a 6.75-inch bore for the 18-36 G. However, the 18-36 G was still classified as a 3-4 plow tractor and retained the 2-speed transmission with forward speeds of 2 and 3 mph. The famous winged Hart-Parr radiator cap, with wings extending from each side of a form shaped like a radiator, made its appearance during the late G series models.

This Hart-Parr 18-36 is equipped with the winged radiator cap, the larger oval fuel tank, wheels with the flat spokes, and the return of the longer rear fenders.

The major revision for the 18-36 H was a new 3-speed transmission which provided forward speeds of 2.3, 3.3, and 4.1 mph and a speed of 2.3 mph in reverse. The 18-36 H retained the 6.75- x 7.00-inch engine, but used a new type of piston for greater compression and power. Also the engine was advertised as a 3-fuel engine, suitable for gasoline, distillate, or kerosene.

The appearance of the 18-36 H was revised with an oval fuel tank with 12 gallons more capacity and rear fenders which extended down to the level of the operator's platform to better protect the operator from dust and dirt. The 18-36 H model was replaced during 1928 with the 18-36 I, but the differences were minor. Flat spoke rear wheels were added for 1929.

The 18-36 G was tested at the Nebraska Tractor Testing Laboratory, but the 18-36 H and 18-36 I were not. The results of the October 1926 tests were:

Model	Test No.	Type of Test	Drawbar Hp	Belt Hp
Hart-Parr 18-36 G Distillate	128	Rated	18.10	36.53
		Maximum	32.26	42.85

By 1926 the change to power farming was under way and the Hart-Parr Company was advertising the increased income that could be realized on each farm from the crops raised on the acres that were previously required to feed the horses. Also the advertising brochure cited examples of one man with a tractor doing as much work as two or three men with horses and thus eliminating the wages, room, and board for one or two hired men.

Matching that trend was the new 12-24 G with an increase in engine size to a 5.75-inch bore — .25 inches larger than the replaced 12-24 E. The growing popularity of distillate as a fuel resulted in changing all the references about "kerosene" to "kerosene and distillate." The 12-24 G retained the 2-speed transmission with forward speeds of 2.7 and 3.5 mph.

The next version of the 12-24 was the 12-24 H with a new 3-speed transmission with forward speeds of 2.7, 3.3, and 4.3 mph and 2.7 mph in reverse. The 12-24 H also featured improved pistons for higher compression. This combination was advertised as a 3-fuel engine and added gasoline as the third fuel.

The 12-24 H matched the 18-36 H by adding 6 inches to the rear of the operator's platform and then extending the rear fenders down to meet the platform. For 1929 the 12-24 H changed to flat spokes for the rear wheels.

Again only the G series was tested at Nebraska. During the rated belt power test in October 1926, the 12-24 G set a new fuel economy record for Hart-Parr tractors of 10.12 hp-hr/gal.

Hart-Parr 12-24 G & Hart-Parr 12-24 H
1926-1927 & 1927-1930

The Hart-Parr 12-24 H was built to burn three types of fuel and was rated as a 2-3 plow tractor. A 3-speed transmission increased its versatility.

Model	Test No.	Type of Test	Drawbar Hp	Belt Hp
Hart-Parr 12-24 G Distillate	129	Rated	12.11	24.09
		Maximum	21.78	31.99

The First Independent PTO
1928 - 1930

With the trend to power farming, many of the implements were redesigned to include a PTO drive. An earlier version of the Hart-Parr PTO attachment was driven with a belt drive from the tractor's belt pulley. Thus this PTO stopped whenever the travel of the tractor was stopped.

The improved PTO attachment for the 12-24 and 18-36 models was driven directly from the right end of the crankshaft and had its own clutch with a control lever mounted at the top of the right fender. Thus it was the first independent PTO, beating the Oliver 88 and the Cockshutt 30 by almost 20 years. The advertising material emphasized the independent control by stating, "should the pulled implement become clogged or overloaded, the operator can stop the tractor and operate the implement until it is cleared. This Hart-Parr feature is most valuable for perfect power take-off operation."

This improved PTO attachment was built to transmit the rated power of the tractor's engine and could be used with pulled or stationary implements. The band type of clutch operated at the end of the crankshaft and the power was transmitted with an enclosed roller chain drive to a cross shaft under the tractor. The cross shaft was connected to a bevel gear box which in turn powered the shaft which passed over the operator's platform and became the connecting point for the implement's PTO shaft. The jaws for cranking the tractor's engine were relocated from the counterweight to the outside of the PTO attachment.

The "chain drive" PTO for the 12-24 and 18-36 was driven directly from the engine crankshaft and controlled with its own clutch, thus making it an independent PTO.

NOTICE THE UNUSUAL CONSTRUCTION SIMPLE—ACCESSIBLE—AND IT DOES DO THE JOB IN A BETTER WAY.

Extension Power Shaft Coupling

Power Take Off Clutch Lever Within Reach Of Operator

Dust Proof Oil Tight Enclosure

Bolted Rigidly To Frame

Independent Clutch Band Operating On Crankshaft Counterweight

Hart-Parr 28-50
1927-1930

The 28-50, which replaced the 22-40, was the last Hart-Parr model to be introduced. Hart-Parr advertised that it had "surplus power" of 64 percent on the drawbar and 29 percent on the belt. This was the difference in the results of the maximum power tests at Nebraska and the tractor's 28-50 rating.

The 28-50 continued to use a 4-cylinder Hart-Parr "Twin-Two" power plant, but now it was built from two of the 12-24 H blocks with a 5.75- x 6.50-inch bore and stroke. This 674-cubic-inch engine had a rated engine speed of 850 rpm which matched that of the 12-24 H. A Madison-Kipp force-feed lubricator provided fresh oil to the pistons and bearings.

The 28-50 weighed about 8,600 pounds and was powered with a 4-cylinder engine which was built from two of the 12-24 H engine blocks.

Two versions of the 28-50 were available, based on the size of the radiator. The narrow version was replaced during 1928 with a wider one, with two indentations on each side of the top casting and a revised mounting to the main frame of the tractor. The wider version was topped with the winged Hart-Parr radiator cap.

The 28-50 retained its 2-speed transmission with forward speeds of 2.2 and 3.3 mph. However, a 3-speed transmission was optional. The 28-50 was equipped with a dry-plate disc clutch and the final drive was enclosed. The 52-inch diameter rear wheels now rotated on a stationary axle.

The fuel efficiency record set by the 12-24 G didn't last long because the 28-50 topped it with 10.73 hp-hr/gal during its rated belt power test in August 1927. The power results were:

Model	Test No.	Type of Test	Drawbar Hp	Belt Hp
Hart-Parr 28-50 Distillate	140	Rated	28.52	50.35
		Maximum	46.03	64.56

17

The New Oliver Tractors

Oliver Chilled Plow Works Tractor
1926-1929

During the mid-1920s the change to power farming was under way as farmers were replacing some of their horses with the smaller, lighter tractors which had become available. The Farmall Regular had been introduced and it was proving to be the answer to the question of how to use a tractor for cultivating. At the same time the trade magazines were discussing why farm machinery dealers needed to carry a complete line of equipment and the advantages of dealing with a full-line company instead of several specialized companies.

Undoubtedly as a result of these trends, the Oliver Chilled Plow Works of South Bend, Indiana, one of the leading manufacturers of plows and other tillage tools, began developing a tractor which was suitable for row-crop work. Although the starting date of this project is not known, later references by the trade magazines indicated the test work started early in 1926. And it is known an experimental tractor was shipped to Texas in 1926 for test work.

By May 1928 the double vertical ring rear wheel had been replaced with the single ring type which later was named the "Tip-Toe" wheel. This 4-row planter was one of the mid-mounted implements developed at the same time as the tractor.

(Photo courtesy of Northern Indiana Historical Society and Studebaker National Museum.)

The first company photographs of the experimental Oliver Chilled Plow Works tractor were taken July 16 and October 29, 1927. This 1927 fall plowing scene illustrates the single front wheel, the double vertical ring rear wheels, the splined rear axles for rear wheel adjustment, and the PTO shaft below the seat.
(Photo courtesy of Northern Indiana Historical Society and Studebaker National Museum.)

The early experimental tractors were built for row-crop work with a single front wheel with a concave rim and two large diameter rear wheels. The rear wheels were adjustable on the splined straight rear axles to fit the row width and provide ample crop clearance. The tractor was powered with a 4-cylinder, L-head type Hercules engine which was positioned vertically with the crankshaft in line with the tractor. The transmission provided three forward speeds and one in reverse.

The earliest photographs of this experimental tractor show each rear wheel consisted of two large diameter, narrow vertical rings with interconnecting cross bars. Lugs were attached to the rings and extended beyond the outside diameter. However, this style of wheel experienced problems of packing sticky soil between the cross bars, so they were replaced with a single vertical ring wheel with attached lugs. And thus was born the rear wheel which would be later known as the "Tip-Toe" wheel.

Since the tractor was designed by an implement company, mid-mounted implements were designed and tested along with the tractor. These implements were mounted to two cross pipes which passed through two cross holes in the tractor's frame. This idea for attaching mid-mounted implements was patented and would be used for many years.

The next build of experimental tractors looked more like a production tractor with the Oliver name cast into the side of the radiator. However, they still were very difficult to service, probably because they were built primarily to determine how well they functioned in a variety of field conditions. The combination frame and crankcase had only a drain hole, so

This June 1928 cultivating scene shows the position of the operator relative to the steering wheel and the foot rests. It also shows the two cross pipes which passed through the tractor and served as the mounting frame for the mid-mounted implements.

(Photo courtesy of Northern Indiana Historical Society and Studebaker National Museum.)

By October 5, 1928, the second build of experimental tractors included the Oliver name on the side of the radiator and fenders for the rear wheels. Also they were painted in two colors, using gray for the tractor and red for the wheels and implements.

(Photo courtesy of Northern Indiana Historical Society and Studebaker National Museum.)

the engine had to be disassembled to check or adjust the bearings. The transmission could be checked only by removing the PTO, seat, and steering assembly from the top of the transmission and rear axle case.

The next generation of this experimental tractor may have been a "pilot run" because the row-crop version was identified as the Model A and other photographs show a standard-tread version with smaller rear

wheels and a fixed width front axle which was labeled the Model B. These tractors had an access plate bolted to the bottom of the crankcase for service and inspection. However, it appears no major changes were made in the transmission and rear axle area to improve the serviceability. It is not known how many of this version were built, but photographs show flat car loads being shipped.

The third version of the row-crop tractor was equipped with an access plate on the bottom of the crankcase and was identified as the Model A. This first photograph of a shipment of Oliver tractors was taken December 15, 1928. Two other shipments were photographed on December 28, 1928, and January 18, 1929.

(Photo courtesy of Northern Indiana Historical Society and Studebaker National Museum.)

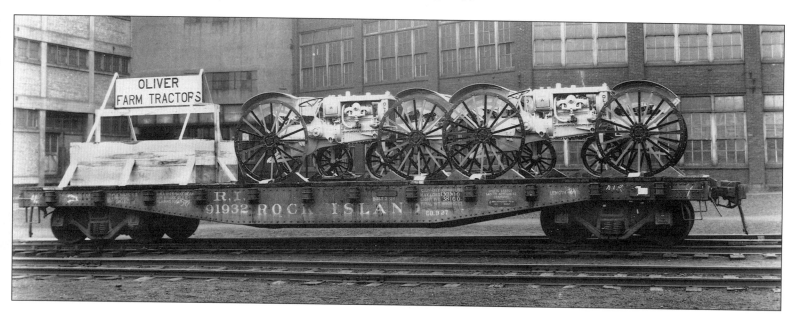

The standard-tread version, named the Model B, was photographed in the field on November 13, 1928, and then later in the studio. Since the corss holes for the row-crop implements are present, it appears this version was created by installing smaller rear wheels, a fixed-tread axle, and redesigned fenders.
(Photo courtesy of Northern Indiana Historical Society and Studebaker National Museum.)

Since the Oliver Chilled Plow Works tractor was an experimental model, it was not tested at the Nebraska Tractor Testing Laboratory. Doug Strawser, a collector in Illinois, found one of the second build experimental tractors in Texas and has restored it.

This picture was taken January 31, 1929, and it may have been anticipating the forthcoming merger. Notice the color scheme has been revised with the tractor now painted a darker color with the letters and lines being a lighter color.

(Photo courtesy of Northern Indiana Historical Society and Studebaker National Museum.)

A Major Merger
1929

The farm equipment industry changed on April 2, 1929, with the creation of another full-line company, the Oliver Farm Equipment Company. This new company was created by the merger of three companies — the Oliver Chilled Plow Works, the Hart-Parr Company, and the Nichols & Shepard Company.

The trade magazines said the terms of the merger were announced on February 22 by J. D. Oliver, president of Oliver Chilled Plow Works; M. W. Ellis, president of Hart-Parr; and L. J. Brown, president of Nichols & Shepard. The stockholders of the individual companies voted on March 29 to dissolve their companies and become part of the new corporation. The officers of the new company were J. D. Oliver, chairman; J. T. Nichols, vice chairman; and M. W. Ellis, president. The executive offices were established at 400 West Madison Street in Chicago.

On May 17, 1929, the Oliver Farm Equipment Company expanded with the merger of the fourth company, the American Seeding Machine Company. And on July 27, 1929, the McKenzie potato machinery line was purchased. Except for hay tools, the Oliver Farm Equipment Company now represented a complete line of farm machinery.

The new corporation announced plans during the summer of 1929 for construction of additional facilities at the tractor factory in Charles City, Iowa. The stated reason for this expansion was the 56 percent increase in 1929 year-to-date sales of Hart-Parr tractors over the similar period of 1928. However, the real reason for this expansion became obvious in 1930.

During 1929 the company's sales efforts were somewhat hampered by the reorganization of the divisions into one company and the reassignment of personnel. However, at the end of 1929 the sales of the new Oliver Farm Equipment Company placed it in a tie with J. I. Case for third place in the farm equipment industry, behind International Harvester and Deere & Company.

The new Oliver flag and shield were used to publicize the new company name while attempting to maintain the loyalty of the customers of the four previous companies.

Oliver Hart-Parr Row Crop
1930-1937

When the Oliver Hart-Parr Row Crop model was introduced in February 1930, the trade magazines said the tractor was developed by the Oliver division for three years and then in the fourth year, 1929, it was turned over to the Hart-Parr division for the final redesign, testing, and production planning. It appears that during this fourth year the general configuration of the Oliver Chilled Plow tractor was combined with an experimental Hart-Parr drive train and a new valve-in-head engine which was being developed by Waukesha. In fact, the prototype tractors built in 1929 were powered with a Waukesha L-head type of engine which is visible in some of the field scenes in the early advertising for the Row Crop.

The Row Crop tractor, with the Oliver name in small letters and the Hart-Parr name in large letters on the front of the radiator, started a new era for tractors manufactured in the Charles City, Iowa, factory. The engine was a vertical type with 4-cylinders and the crankshaft was in-line with the chassis of the tractor. The general purpose configuration used a single wheel with a concave rim in front and two large

In 1931 the single front wheel was replaced with two closely spaced wheels. A rod on each side of the tractor's frame engaged one of the brakes when the front wheels were turned.

The first Oliver Hart-Parr tractor was the Row Crop with two cross holes in its frame for attaching implements. Pictured here is one of the 1929 prototypes with the L-head engine.

59.5-inch diameter wheels which attached to the straight rear axle for ample crop clearance. These rear wheels were only .56-inches wide, so they were just a base for attaching the lugs which in turn provided the traction and supported the weight of the tractor. Oliver described these wheels as the Tip-Toe design. Wheel spacing was adjustable from 60 to 74 inches by sliding the wheels on the axle.

The Row Crop used the unique system for attaching mid-mounted implements to the tractor which had been developed for the Oliver Chilled Plow tractor. Two cross holes were provided in the body of the tractor, one in the lower crankcase below the fan and one in the transmission casting. A cross pipe was placed in each of these holes and then the implements, such as a planter or cultivator, were attached to these pipes.

The engine for the Row Crop, with an operating speed of 1,150 rpm, was started on gasoline and then operated on kerosene. Oliver described the power plant as their engine, but it was a Waukesha design which was jointly manufactured by Waukesha and the Hart-Parr division of Oliver. The sliding spur gear transmission provided three forward speeds of 2.6, 3.2, and 4.1 mph and one in reverse. The clutch pedal was located on the

This section view of the Row Crop or 18-27 illustrates the production valve-in-head engine which resulted in a close fit between the engine and hood. The basic design of this power train was used in all three models introduced in 1930.

right side of the operator's station and a lever operated the brake on the bull pinion.

The belt pulley was standard equipment and was now located on the right side of the tractor. The 553 rpm PTO was optional and was driven by the transmission from the same powertrain as the belt pulley. The mounted implements were counterbalanced with springs and were raised and lowered with hand levers.

During 1931 the Row Crop was improved by replacing the 29-inch diameter single front wheel with a tricycle front end with 24-inch dual wheels and the addition of individual foot-operated differential shaft brakes to assist in turning. A rod and lever mechanism also automatically

engaged these brakes when the front wheels were turned. Axle-type brakes were field installed on many of the earlier Row Crops. By 1934 a wide front axle was available and the size of the names on the radiator had been reversed. Oliver was now in large letters and Hart-Parr was the smaller size name.

After the Nebraska Tractor Test which was conducted in April 1930, the Row Crop was also known as the 18-27. The results of the test, with kerosene as the fuel, were:

Model	Test No.	Type of Test	Drawbar Hp	Belt Hp
Oliver Hart-Parr Row Crop	176	Rated	18.10	27.11
		Maximum	24.40	29.72

The next size in the new line of Oliver Hart-Parr tractors with vertical 4-cylinder engines was introduced in July 1930. It was first named the 2-3 plow tractor and became the 18-28 after being tested at Nebraska. It was a standard-tread version of the 18-27 Row Crop. The rear wheels were 44 inches in diameter, 10 inches wide, and a variety of lugs were available.

Oliver Hart-Parr 18-28
1930-1937

The 18-28 used the same 280-cubic-inch engine and 3-speed transmission as the 18-27 Row Crop, but the rated engine speed was increased to 1,190 rpm. This resulted in the one additional horsepower for its belt power rating and, when combined with a different gear ratio, permitted the 18-28 with its smaller rear wheels to have the same travel speeds of 2.6, 3.2, and 4.1 mph as the Row Crop. The belt pulley was standard equipment and the PTO shaft with a speed of 572 rpm was optional. In 1931 the Orchard version was added with a lowered seat and steering wheel, tapered fenders which covered the upper half of the rear wheels, sheet metal disks for the front wheels, and a redirected exhaust pipe. Other versions for specific applications were available by 1934 such as the Western Special with a special air cleaner and the Rice Special with special wheel lugs.

The 18-28 was tested at Nebraska in July 1930 with kerosene. A fuel efficiency of 10.00 hp-hr/gal was achieved during the rated belt power test. The other test results were:

The Oliver Hart-Parr 18-28 was a standard-tread version of the 18-27 Row Crop. Its slightly faster engine speed resulted in one more belt horsepower.

Model	Test No.	Type of Test	Drawbar Hp	Belt Hp
Oliver Hart-Parr 18-28	180	Rated	18.99	28.30
		Maximum	23.56	30.29

Oliver Hart-Parr 28-44
1930-1937

The third new model was a larger standard-tread tractor which was rated as a 3-5 plow tractor. It was introduced in June 1930 as the Model A, but later was named the 28-44. A wide variety of lugs were available for the 46-inch diameter rear wheels with a 12-inch width.

The 28-44 used a vertical 4-cylinder, valve-in-head engine which was based on a Waukesha design, but was manufactured by the Hart-Parr division of Oliver. To develop the increased power, it had a 4.75-inch bore and a 6.25-inch stroke for a displacement of 443 cubic inches. The rated speed was 1,125 rpm. The 3-speed transmission provided speeds of 2.2, 3.3, and 4.3 mph. The clutch pedal was located on the right side of the operator's station and the brake lever was on the left.

The power-train for the 28-44 was similar to its smaller brothers.

The largest model introduced in 1930 was the 28-44. This standard-tread tractor with its 443-cubic-inch engine was rated as a 3-5 plow tractor.

The belt pulley was standard equipment and the PTO was optional. Other optional equipment was used to create different versions of the 28-44 such as the Western Special, the Rice Field Special, and the Tip-Toe Rice Field Special. The Thresherman's Special, which weighed 10,550 pounds, was equipped with a chime whistle and solid cast disc wheels. In 1936 a High Compression Special was introduced with a higher compression engine which burned gasoline and was factory rated as a 32-50.

In October 1930 the 28-44 was tested at Nebraska and recorded a fuel economy of 10.42 hp-hr/gal of kerosene during the rated belt power test. The power test results were:

Model	Test No.	Type of Test	Drawbar Hp	Belt Hp
Oliver Hart-Parr 28-44	183	Rated	28.44	44.29
		Maximum	34.21	49.04

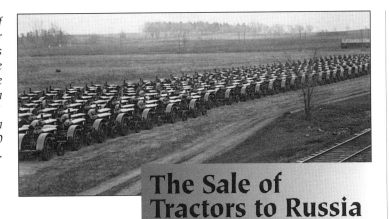

These rows of Oliver Hart-Parr 28-44 tractors are thought to be a portion of the tractors built in 1930 and 1931 for the Russian order of 5,000 tractors.

The Sale of Tractors to Russia
1930-1931

During August 1930, while production was starting on the 28-44, the factory manager and some of his engineering and service people were at the Experimental Farm near Charles City. They were assisting a delegation from Russia testing one of the new 28-44 models in as tough of field conditions as could be found. Evidently the tests were successful because the *Wall Street Journal* reported the Russians placed a $12 million order for 5,000 of the large tractors, 1,500 combines built by the Nichols & Shepard division, and $1 million of implements. A later production schedule listed 5,000 tractors and 2,000 combines.

From September through November 1930, production of the 28-44 gradually increased from 21 to over 40 per day. By December the production rate of the 28-44 tractors was 50 or more per day compared to eight or nine for the Row Crop and five for the 18-28. Starting on November 1 the factory started shipping 40 of the 28-44 tractors per day and then shipments increased to a variation of 40, 60, or 80 per day.

Production continued at the rate of over 50 per day until February 20, 1931, when only 40 were built. Then production of the 28-44 model stopped until April 28 when one tractor was built. The same dramatic shift happened with shipments of the 28-44 which continued at the rate of 40 or 80 per day until February 21 when it suddenly changed to an occasional four or six.

In 1931 Merle Tucker, who later became a vice president for Oliver, and a staff of 16 men were sent to Russia for over a year to teach the Russians how to operate the machines. When the U.S. ambassador to Russia returned in 1937, his art collection included a painting, dated 1931, which depicted an Oliver 28-44 tractor and combine harvesting grain while a group of women shoveled the dumped grain into sacks and loaded them onto a cart pulled by two camels.

Oliver Hart-Parr 70
1935-1937

Introduced in the fall of 1935, the 2-plow Oliver Hart-Parr Row Crop 70 ushered in a new era in tractor design for the major tractor companies with its new styling and a 6-cylinder engine. It featured a grill over the radiator, engine side panels, and a double plowshare radiator cap. This additional tractor model for the Oliver line still displayed both names above the grill.

Two versions of the Row Crop 70 were available, one with a high compression (HC) engine for 70-octane gasoline (the reason for the 70 model number) and a second with a KD engine for use with kerosene or distillate. Different cylinder heads and manifolds were used to obtain the two versions. The new valve-in-head engine, built by Continental to Oliver's specifications, had a displacement of 201 cubic inches. The operating speed was 1,500 rpm.

The 4-speed transmission provided three working speeds of 2.4, 3.3, and 4.3 mph, plus a road speed of 5.9 mph. The mid-mounted implements were carried on two cross pipes which passed through the tractor's frame. The power lift, PTO, and belt pulley were optional.

The seat was a unique rod frame and hammock type. The clutch pedal moved to the left side. Foot pedals for the differential brakes were located on each side of the transmission. Lights and an electric starter were optional.

Two additional models of the Oliver Hart-Parr 70 were announced in the summer of 1936. One was the Standard 70 and the second model was the Orchard 70 with fenders which covered the top half of the rear wheels.

The Nebraska tests now listed "corrected horsepower" to adjust for the temperature and barometric pressure. On this basis the Row Crop 70 HC developed 22.58 drawbar horsepower and 29.56 belt horsepower during its April 1936 tests instead of being a 16-25 model with the old rating system.

"New for 1936," the Oliver Hart-Parr 70 provided the choice of Tip-Toe steel wheels or 8.25-40 rear rubber tires.

Oliver 70
1937-1948

On October 15, 1937, the Oliver dealers in all 48 states removed the whitewash from their display windows and uncovered a canvas-draped tractor on the showroom floor to reveal a restyled Oliver 70 tractor. For the next 70 days, to match the model number, a national advertising campaign was conducted to inform all farmers of this new model which now carried only the Oliver name.

It was described as a "streamliner" with its oval grill and engine side panels with long, horizontal louvers. Emphasis was placed on its modern automotive design with a smooth running 6-cylinder engine designed specifically for the fuel it was to use, operator convenience with its automotive steering and electric starter, and the streamline appearance.

The Oliver 70 continued to be available as the Row Crop, the Standard, and the Orchard. The Row Crop could be equipped with dual front wheels, a single front wheel, or a wide front axle which was named the 4-Wheel High Clearance. Rear wheels for the Row Crop 70 included the Tip-Toe

The Oliver 70 with its 6-cylinder engine was called a "streamliner" with its oval grill and engine side panels.

steel wheels or a choice of 9.00-40, 10.00-38, or 11.00-40 rubber tires.

The power train continued to use the HC or KD versions of the 201-cubic-inch engine. However, in 1938 the engine was revised from a 5-gear drive for the camshaft, magneto, and governor to one using three gears. By late 1938 Oliver reported 75 percent of the model 70 tractors were being sold with an electric starter. With the growing popularity of rubber tires, a 6-speed "double neutral" transmission with a top speed of 13.4 mph was optional first and then became standard in 1944. However, the fifth and sixth gears were locked out if the tractor was equipped with steel wheels. By 1947 the hammock type of seat had been replaced with an upholstered spring seat, the throttle lever had moved to the steering column, and the rear tire sizes for the Row Crop 70 had changed to 11.00-38 and 12.00-38. These two sizes were later reidentified as 12.4-38 and 13.6-38 when the tire industry changed from tread width to sidewall width.

A Standard 70 with a completely enclosed cab was exhibited at Wichita's Western Tractor and Power Equipment Show in February 1939. A padded cushion was attached to the inside of the large rear door which made a back rest for the seat when the door was closed. Later Raby

Visitors to the Oliver display at the 1937 state fairs voted for their favorite color combination from the six examples on display. The selections included green with red trim, green with orange trim, red with aluminum trim, yellow with black trim, gold with orange trim, and ivory with gold trim. Evidently the green with red trim won because the new 70 was painted Oliver green with red wheels and a red stripe on the frame. The grill was first plated a silver color and then changed to yellow paint.

Six different colored tractors were used in Oliver's 1937 color survey.

The Row Crop 70 could be equipped with a steel cab built by Raby Mfg.

Manufacturing made a steel cab for the Row Crop 70 with a smaller rear door and a back panel. The side windows raised and lowered with web straps and buckles.

The Oliver Row Crop 70 with the high compression engine, 6-speed transmission, and rubber tires was tested at Nebraska in August 1940. This tractor provided an excellent example of the different test results which could be obtained from the Nebraska Tractor Tests. The "maximum" listed below is the observed maximum power during the test and the "corrected" refers to the maximum values after being corrected to a standard temperature and barometric pressure. Of course the tractor manufacturers preferred to use the corrected power results.

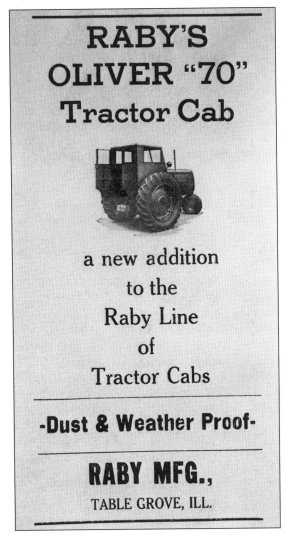
Model	Test No.	Type of Test	Drawbar Hp	Belt Hp
Row Crop 70 Gasoline	351	Corrected	30.18	33.38
		Maximum	28.63	31.52
		Rated	22.72	28.46

Oliver 80
1937-1948

Late in 1937 the Oliver 80 was introduced as the replacement for the 18-27 Row Crop and the 18-28 Standard models. The new 80 was built in a row-crop and standard-tread configuration and was now rated as a full 3-plow tractor. Although the 80 followed the 70's concept of having two versions of the basic valve-in-head engine for the two types of fuel, it retained the plain appearance and 4-cylinder engine design of the 18-27 and 18-28.

To provide the full 3-plow rating, both versions of the Waukesha-Oliver engine had a rated speed of 1,200 rpm and a larger bore size than the replaced engine, being 4.25 inches for the HC and 4.50 inches for the KD. This resulted in displacements of 298 and 334 cubic inches which provided similar tractor power from the two kinds of fuel.

Both the row-crop and standard-tread versions could be equipped with the same sizes of steel wheels used on the 18-27 and 18-28. Rubber tires also were available with the rear tire size being 11.25-24 and 12.75-24 for the standard-tread version and 11.25-40 and 11.25-42 for the row-crop version. The row-crop tractor also could be equipped with an adjustable high clearance front axle and a power lift for the mounted implements. Extra equipment included a PTO and an electric starter for the Standard

This Oliver 80 had the larger upper radiator tank and larger fuel tank. This change also increased the space between the top of the engine and the hood.

80. Due to potential interference with the mid-mounted implements, the Row Crop 80 was not redesigned to permit adding an electric starter.

Two major changes were made during the production of the model 80. In 1938 the hood line was raised which increased the size of the upper tank of the radiator and enlarged the main fuel tank from 13 to 17 gallons. The transmission was changed from three forward speeds to four during 1938 for the Standard and during 1939 for the Row Crop.

The Standard 80 was the only HC version tested at Nebraska. In Test 365 conducted in November 1940, the 4-speed version with rubber tires produced a corrected maximum 36.88 drawbar horsepower and a corrected maximum 42.43 belt horsepower.

Oliver 90 & 99
1937-1952

The Oliver 90 and 99 models could be built with steel wheels which in turn could be equipped with many different types of lugs.

The 28-44 was updated in late 1937 with a 4-speed transmission and was reidentified as the model 90. The 90 retained the 3-fuel engine, capable of burning gasoline, kerosene, or distillate. However, the former High Compression Special with the engine built for only gasoline was now known as the model 99. The 90 was rated as a 4-plow tractor and in 1937 the 99 was described as "the most powerful 4-wheel tractor built" and carried a 5-plow rating. Except for new engine side panels, both the 90 and 99 retained the plain styling of the 28-44.

The Oliver 99 with its high compression engine replaced the High Compression Special and was equipped with a new 4-speed transmission and new engine side panels.

Both 4-cylinder Oliver-built engines had a 4.75-inch bore, a 6.25-inch stroke, and a rated speed of 1,125 rpm. The new 4-speed transmission retained the 2.2, 3.3, and 4.3 mph speeds and added a road speed of 5.5 mph. By 1950 this had been revised to be 2.5, 3.8, 5.0 and 6.5 mph with an optional speed of 13.5 mph to replace the 6.5.

Originally the rear wheel equipment included 46-inch diameter steel wheels with a width of 12 inches or two sizes of rubber tires, 12.75-28 or 13.25-28. By 1950 the rubber tires had changed to 13-30, 14-30, or 15-30 (14.9-30, 16.9-30, or 18.4-30 using the later designations). Optional equipment included the PTO, electric lights, and an electric starter.

For 1950 the production of the 90 and 99 was moved from Charles City to the South Bend Plant Number 2. Their first change was increasing the compression ratio to 5.5 to 1. Then the traditional fenders which extended over the wheels were replaced with the clam shell type, so larger rubber tires could be installed. Also the rubber torsion spring type of seat was added for improved operator comfort. Double disc steering brakes were installed on the rear axle and the clutch pedal was relocated to the left side.

The 90 was not tested at Nebraska, although its output would have been similar to Test 183 for the 28-44. The 99's performance was measured by Test 451 in October 1950. The corrected maximum drawbar power was 54.57 horsepower and the corrected maximum belt power was 63.87 horsepower.

The Oliver 60 matched the streamlined appearance of the model 70, but operator comfort was improved.

The Standard 60 was introduced in 1942 with a 4-speed transmission. In 1944 it was changed to five forward speeds.

Oliver 60
1940-1948

Oliver entered the "small" tractor market in late 1940 with their new Row Crop 60. This 2-row, 1-2 plow tractor featured the same styling as the 70 and the same implement mounting system with two cross pipes passing through the 60's pressed steel frame. The row-crop version of the 60 was the tricycle type with two closely spaced front wheels. Later, in 1942, a standard version was added and by 1947 an adjustable front axle was available for the Row Crop 60.

The 60 was equipped with a 4-cylinder, high compression engine with 120.6-cubic-inch displacement. This jointly developed and manufactured Waukesha-Oliver engine had a bore and stroke of 3.31 inches and 3.50 inches. The first sliding spur gear transmission provided four forward speeds, ranging from 2.65 to 6.25 mph.

The tractor could be equipped with either rubber tires or the Tip-Toe steel wheels. Other optional equipment included a PTO, a 2-speed belt pulley, a power lift, fenders, an electric starter, and electric lights.

The trend toward operator comfort and convenience was emphasized with an adjustable, upholstered spring seat and a high-mounted operator's station for visibility. All the gauges and switches were located on the inclined dash.

The Row Crop 60 was revised in 1944 to provide two brake pedals which were connected with an equalizer bar for applying both brakes at road speeds. Also the transmission was revised to provide a fifth forward speed and a high speed reverse. It was another "double neutral" transmission, but for the 60 both of the "high" gears were the same speed, so the six forward gears resulted in only five forward speeds.

Many of the design features which were new for the Row Crop 60 became design characteristics for Oliver tractors for many years. These

included the metered oil system for the engine, a flat operator's platform positioned above the powertrain, the two brake pedals with the equalizer bar, the throttle lever on the steering column, and the inclined dash.

The 60 was tested at Nebraska in September 1941 and in Test 375 it developed 17.85 corrected drawbar horsepower and 19.51 corrected horsepower on the belt. Fuel economy was outstanding for this time period with 11.97 hp-hr/gal of gasoline during the belt test.

The inclined dash provided a convenient location for the electric starter button. The power lift was located under the dash.

Oliver 80 Diesel
1940-1947

On July 9, 1940, Oliver started building the first row-crop tractor powered with a diesel engine that was built on a production basis. A 4-cylinder Buda diesel engine was used as the power plant for both the Row Crop 80 and the Standard 80. Production records show Oliver built 28 in 1940, 62 in 1941, 36 in 1942, 1 in 1943, and 9 in 1947. Thus there were a total of 136 Oliver 80 Diesel tractors, 90 of the Row Crops, and 46 of the Standards.

The Buda 4DT226 engine had a 3.00-inch bore and a 5.12-inch stroke for a displacement of 226 cubic inches. The engine used a fuel pump and nozzles built by the Robert Bosch Company and a Lanova combustion chamber. Since the 80's regular frame casting

The Buda diesel engine required a new frame casting which provided space for an electric starter.

was built to also be the crankcase for the Waukesha style of gasoline engine, a new frame casting was required to mount the diesel engine which had its own crankcase. However, the new frame did provide space for an electric starter.

This diesel-powered tractor was not tested at Nebraska. Today a few of the Row Crop 80 Diesel tractors have been found in the United States and at least one of the Standard 80 Diesel units exists in England.

The Oliver 80 Diesel was built in both a Row Crop and Standard version. Both versions were equipped with the small radiator tank and an electric starter.

Oliver HG Crawler
1944-1951

The Oliver tractor line expanded on October 31, 1944, with the purchase of the Cleveland Tractor Company and its line of Cletrac crawlers. The smallest model, the HG, was primarily an agricultural tractor. At this time the company changed its name to the Oliver Corporation.

The Cletrac HG was originally introduced in 1939 with a Hercules 4-cylinder engine which had a 3-inch bore, a 4-inch stroke, and a rated speed of 1,400 rpm. Then in late 1940 the engine was changed to a 3.12-inch bore and a 1,700 rpm rated speed. The 3-speed transmission provided speeds of 2.0, 3.2, and 5.3 mph. The standard tracks were 6 inches wide and had a track tread of 31, 42, or 68 inches. Optional were 8-, 10-, and 12-inch wide tracks.

The Oliver Cletrac HG continued to be built in the Cleveland, Ohio, factory. It was painted Cletrac orange until late 1945 and then Oliver green. In 1950 the engine was changed to a 3.25-inch bore. A 60-inch track tread was added to provide 4 row-width spacings. A front-mounted implement frame which used two caster wheels and the two cross pipes was provided, so Oliver cultivators and similar implements could be attached.

In 1945 the HGR model, a rubber-belted version of the HG, was introduced. However, the rubber used in the belts was not very durable, especially when used in dirt. It appears most of the HGR models were converted back to steel tracks. Some of the HGR-42 tractors survived and are owned by collectors today.

The Oliver HG crawler with the 3.25-inch bore engine was tested at Nebraska in November 1949. In Test 434 it developed 21.85 corrected drawbar horsepower and 26.36 corrected belt horsepower.

A service representative was demonstrating how to install the rubber track on an Oliver HGR crawler.

The Oliver 88 with a 6-cylinder engine, a 6-speed transmission, and an independent PTO was styled to match the 60 and 70 for the first year.

Oliver 88
1947-1948

The Oliver line of tractors began to have more of a family appearance in mid-1947 when the Oliver 88 was introduced to replace the model 80. This new 88, which was produced until mid-1948, had the oval grill and streamline appearance of the 60 and 70 and a 6-cylinder engine like the 70. It was rated as a 3-4 plow tractor and was available in the row-crop and standard-tread configurations.

The only version of engine available for this 88, was the 230.9-cubic-inch Waukesha-Oliver HC engine with a 3.50-inch bore and a 4.00-inch stroke. Rated engine speed was 1,600 rpm. The 6-cylinder engine was combined with a 6-speed, "double neutral" transmission with a speed range of 2.6 to 12.3 mph for the Row Crop version. A 22-gallon fuel tank provided enough capacity to generally eliminate the need to refill during the day.

The outstanding feature of this tractor was the independent PTO which was controlled with its own clutch. Depressing the tractor's clutch pedal to stop forward travel did not stop the implement powered by the PTO, which was a great convenience in clearing an overloaded harvesting machine. Also the optional power lift was independent because it was powered by the same driveline as the PTO.

The standard wheel equipment was now rubber tires, with the rear tires being 11-38 or 12-38 (12.4-38 or 13.6-38 now) for the Row Crop 88 and 12-26 (13.6-26 now) for the Standard 88. The belt pulley was standard for the Standard 88, but was optional for the Row Crop 88.

The results of the tests at Nebraska in late 1947 and early 1948 were:

Model	Test No.	Type of Test	Drawbar Hp	Belt Hp
Row Crop 88 Gasoline	388	Corrected	38.40	44.66
Standard 88 Gasoline	391	Corrected	38.56	44.96

The Fleetlines, the Supers, and the 3-Digit Models

Oliver 66 Fleetline & Oliver 77 & 88 Fleetlines
1949-1954 & 1948-1954

Oliver celebrated its centennial in 1948 by introducing the Fleetline tractor series. The new 66, 77, and restyled 88 represented a family of tractors with many common parts.

The Oliver Corporation traced its ancestry back to 1848 when Nichols & Shepard was originally formed. So on June 30, 1948, Oliver celebrated its centennial by introducing a new line of three tractors with new styling. Billboards across the country illustrated the new 66, 77, and 88 models and described them as the "New Fleet of Quality Tractors." The three models with their new styling came to be known as the Fleetline series.

Except for the new style of hood, grill, and engine side panels, the 88 Fleetline was the same tractor as the 88 introduced in 1947. As a result, some owners of the first style of 88's changed their sheet metal to the fleetline type to have the latest style. Therefore, collectors today sometimes discover their 88 Fleetline has a serial number of one of the more rare first style 88 tractors and convert it back to its original form.

Each of the three models was available in a row-crop or standard-tread configuration and carried this designation on the side of the hood along with its model number. The Row Crop version could be equipped with the common tricycle front end with two closely spaced wheels, an adjustable front axle, or a single front wheel. The Standard versions were soon modified to also provide an Orchard version of each model. The 66 with its 4-cylinder engine was rated as a 2-plow tractor. The 77 was powered with a 6-cylinder version of the 66's engine for a 2-3 plow tractor rating, and the 88 was rated as a 3-4 plow tractor with its larger 6-cylinder engine.

Since the three new models were designed at the same time, they shared many common parts which simplified the manufacturing process and the stock of service parts. The jointly developed and manufactured Waukesha-Oliver gasoline engine for the 77 started with a bore of 3.19 inches and a stroke of 3.75 inches, but the bore was increased to 3.31 inches before the first 66's were produced. With the 3.31-inch bore, the 77's 6-cylinder gasoline engine had a displacement of 193.9 cubic inches and the 4-cylinder gasoline engine in the 66 had 129.3 cubic inches. The 6-cylinder gasoline engine in the 88 had a 3.50-inch bore and a 4.00-inch stroke for a displacement of 230.9 cubic inches. However, it used the same timing gears, rocker arms, governor, oil pump, and other components as the other two engines.

The three engine sizes originally were available in a HC version for gasoline and a KD version for use with kerosene or distillate. The KD versions had a different cylinder head, manifold, carburetor, and a larger bore to provide the same power.

All three models were equipped with sliding spur gear transmissions which used the "double neutral" system to provide six forward speeds and two in reverse with a single gear shift lever. The six forward speeds were evenly spaced, so throttling the engine between 900 and 1,600 rpm and selecting one of the six speeds provided a complete coverage of travel speeds between 1.4 and 11.5 mph.

The 66 and 77 joined the 88 by providing an independent PTO as the only type of PTO drive available. The PTO clutch was controlled with a

The 77 model replaced the popular 70, but retained the 6-cylinder engine and the 6-speed transmission. It featured new styling and an independent PTO.

The Charles City, Iowa, factory expanded by building a new assembly line for the Fleetline series.

hand lever which could be positioned on either the right or left side of the tractor seat.

Two other means of transmitting power were the belt pulley and power lift. The belt pulley could be easily removed if it interfered with the mid-mounted implements. A power lift was provided for raising and lowering cultivators and other similar implements which were carried on the two pipes which passed through the frame of the Row Crops. The power lift was powered by the PTO driveline, so it too operated independently of the travel of the tractor.

The 66 and 77 used a series of stamped steel rear wheels with an attached rim while the 88 was equipped with a cast-iron wheel and a series of bolt-on rims. The Tip-Toe type of steel wheel was still available and was attached to the cast-iron wheel, replacing the bolt-on rim. This combination could also be used on the 66 and 77 models. The rear tire sizes for the Row Crops were based on 38-inch diameter tires: with 8-38, 9-38, or 10-38 tires for the 66; 10-38, 11-38, or 12-38 tires for the 77; and 11-38, 12-38, or 13-38 tires for the 88, using the old tread width system of sizes. The Standard 66 used 24-inch rear tires and the Standard 77 and Standard 88 were equipped with 26-inch tires.

The first tractor seat used on these three models was the the upholstered, spring-type seat which had been used with the 60 and the late 70s. The two brake pedals operated band brakes on the differential shaft and were connected with an equalizer pedal which was located between them.

The Row Crop 77 with its 3.31-inch bore engine was tested at Nebraska in November 1948 and again in September 1949. The Row Crop 66 was tested in June 1949. The 88 was not retested, since its performance had not changed.

Model	Test No.	Type of Test	Drawbar Hp	Belt Hp
Row Crop 66 Gasoline	412	Corrected	22.30	26.05
Row Crop 77 Gasoline	404	Corrected	29.90	35.13
Row Crop 77 Gasoline	425	Corrected	34.20	38.82

Fleetline Improvements
1949-1952

In 1949 Oliver introduced the Ridemaster seat as standard equipment for the 66, 77, and 88 models. The new seat featured two round rubber discs which were used as torsional springs. It was adjustable to provide equal riding qualities for operators ranging from 100 to 275 pounds. The Orchard versions also used this same type of seat, but in a different configuration to provide the lowered position for the operator.

Following World War II, tractor engineers started developing hydraulic systems which could be used to raise and lower both mounted and drawn implements plus control the operating setting.

Oliver's answer to this challenge was the Hydra-lectric system which was introduced in 1950. It used a hydraulic pump, valve, and reservoir unit which mounted to the floor of the operator's platform in the same location as the mechanical power lift and thus it operated independently. The hydraulic system powered one or two double-acting hydraulic cylinders. Instead of a manual control lever, the hydraulic valves were controlled by solenoids which in turn were controlled by electric switches mounted on the steer-

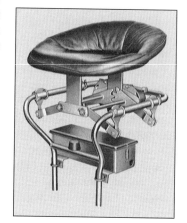

The Ridemaster seat was a popular Oliver feature for many years.

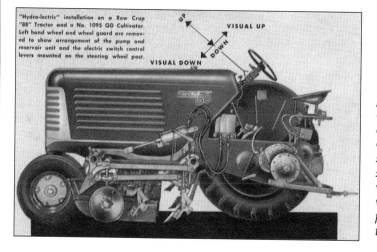

The Hydra-lectric system permitted the operator to adjust the cylinder depth stops while seated, the visual up and visual down functions in the diagram.

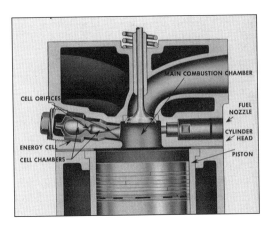

The Oliver diesel engines used the Lanova combustion system with its unique energy cell, on the left side above, which permitted starting on diesel fuel.

ing column. An electromagnet on the rod end of the hydraulic cylinder provided the depth setting and could be relocated by the operator from the tractor seat. Although the system offered many advantages, it was susceptible to problems caused by dust and rain. By 1952 Oliver also offered the same hydraulic system with manual control levers which eliminated the electrical controls and wiring. However, this system also required a manually adjusted stop on the hydraulic cylinder.

In 1949 Oliver made 6-cylinder diesel engines available for the 77 and 88 tractors and later added a 4-cylinder diesel engine for the 66. The diesel engines had the same bore and stroke as the HC (gasoline) engines and were designed to provide approximately the same horsepower. The engines featured the Lanova combustion system which provided easier starting and more efficient burning of the fuel and air mixture. The starting mechanism was powered by a 12-volt electrical system and offered the convenience of starting on diesel fuel alone. An electric coil in the intake manifold preheated the air if the temperature was below freezing. These diesel engines were available when farmers began to understand the economies of using diesel fuel and by 1956 Oliver was advertising that it was making 43 percent of all the diesel tractors on wheels.

As LP gas became more available as a tractor fuel, it became the most economical fuel in many areas. Therefore, factory-built LP gas engines were made available in 1951 for the 77 and 88 tractors.Another improvement added in 1951 for the 88 and in 1952 for the 66 and 77 was double disc brakes. These brakes provided equal holding power in forward or reverse. The braking effort required was about 50 percent less than with the previous band brakes.

By 1952 a Hydra-Lift Hitch was available for use with 3-point hitch implements. A hydraulic cylinder was used to raise the implement, but the weight of the implement was used for lowering. Thus a plow was free to float and maintain a constant working depth. A turnbuckle was built into the top link to tilt the implement from front to back and thus regulate the initial working depth.

Oliver 99 Styled
1952-1953

After producing the Oliver 99 with its plain styling for three years in South Bend Plant Number 2, Oliver announced a revised 99 with a 6-cylinder engine and styling similar to the Fleetlines. However, this 99 was not equipped with engine side panels. The 4-speed transmission was retained, so only the front half of the tractor was revised. This new 99 was rated by Oliver as a 4-5 plow tractor with 65 horsepower on the belt.

This new 99 offered a choice of a gasoline or a diesel Waukesha-Oliver 6-cylinder engine, each with a 4.00-inch stroke and a 4.00-inch bore. The resulting displacement was 302 cubic inches and the rated engine speed was 1,675 rpm. The diesel engine was called a "full diesel" because it started on diesel fuel. Both engines featured the metered lubrication system to reduce oil consumption.

Late in 1952 the Oliver 99 was revised to include the Fleetline type of styling and a choice of a 6-cylinder gasoline or diesel engine.

When the 4-speed transmission was combined with the standard 14-30 (16.9-30 now) rear tires, the speeds were 2.6, 3.8, 5.1, and 13.6 mph. Since the drivetrain was not revised, the PTO was not independent, stopping whenever the tractor's clutch was disengaged. The belt pulley was smaller due to the increased engine speed, but was still located on the right side of the tractor.

Operator comfort and convenience were becoming more important for this size of tractor, so Oliver's advertising emphasized the Saginaw recirculating ball steering system, the rubber torsion spring seat, and the double disc, rear axle steering brakes. A hydraulic system for operating a remote hydraulic cylinder could be added with the pump mounted at the front of the engine.

This model 99 with a 6-cylinder engine and a 4-speed transmission was not tested at the Nebraska Tractor Testing Laboratory.

Oliver OC-3 Crawler & Oliver OC-6 Crawler
1951-1957 & 1953-1960

In 1951 the Oliver OC-3 crawler replaced the HG crawler. The OC-3 model was basically the same as the HG, using 6-inch wide tracks with four track treads of 31, 42, 60, and 68 inches. Also 8- and 10-inch wide tracks were available for all four track treads and 12-inch wide tracks could be used with the 60- and 68-inch sizes. The OC-3 continued to be powered by a Hercules 4-cylinder gasoline engine with a 3.25-inch bore and a 4-inch stroke. The transmission provided three forward speeds and one in reverse. The OC-3 cited the HG's Nebraska Test 434 for its power ratings of 21.85 drawbar horsepower and 26.36 horsepower on the belt.

The OC-6 Crawler, which was announced in 1953, was derived from the model 77 wheel tractor. The OC-6 was rated as a 3-plow tractor with its 6-cylinder engine and 6-speed transmission. It was offered in four track treads of 32, 42, 60, and 68 inches to fit a variety of row spacings. The standard track width was 8 inches, but 10 and 12 inch widths also were available. Crop clearance was 20 inches.

Both the gasoline and diesel 6-cylinder engines were the ones used in the model 77, with a 3.31-inch bore, a 3.75-inch stroke, and a rated speed of 1,600 rpm. Later the bore of the gasoline engine was increased to 3.50 inches to match the change in the wheel tractors. The transmission provided six forward speeds, ranging from 1.9 mph to 8.9 mph.

Optional equipment included an independent PTO, the Hydra-Lift Hitch for 3-point hitch implements, and an independent hydraulic system for one or two remote hydraulic cylinders. A belt pulley was not available for the OC-6.

The OC-6 was tested at Nebraska in April and May 1954. The gasoline version was rated at 32.99 drawbar horsepower and the diesel at 34.74 drawbar horsepower, corrected to sea level.

The Oliver OC-6 crawler used the same 6-cylinder gasoline and diesel engines as the Oliver 77 wheel tractor .

Oliver XO-121 Tractor
1954

Gasoline octane ratings had increased from 70 in 1936 to the lower 80s by 1954, so the Oliver tractor engineers decided to determine what performance could be expected with a much higher compression engine and a corresponding higher octane rating of gasoline. In 1954 they built an experimental Oliver tractor with a compression ratio of 12 to 1, hence the XO-121 designation.

The tractor used an Oliver 88 chassis and was equipped with a 4-cylinder gasoline engine built from a Hercules diesel engine block. It had a 3.75-inch bore and a 4.50-inch stroke with a rated speed of 1,600 rpm. The Ethyl Corporation provided the experimental fuel which had a rating beyond the conventional octane scale, but was estimated to be in the 101 to 107 range.

The experimental engine was tested on an engine dynamometer, in belt performance tests and in field drawbar work. It proved to be functional and practical and was described as the most efficient tractor engine ever built at that time. The results of the belt tests were:

The Oliver XO-121 was built to determine the performance of a gasoline engine with a 12 to 1 compression ratio.

	70	77	XO-121
Engine Displacement (cu. in.)	201	194	199
Compression Ratio	6.50:1	6.75:1	12.0:1
Governed Engine Speed (rpm)	1,500	1,600	1,600
HP, Corrected Maximum	29.56	38.82	56.90
Efficiency at max. Hp (hp-hr/gal)	11.07	11.73	15.50

For the XO-121, the traditional Oliver colors were reversed with the body painted red and the wheels green. A chrome grill with vertical slots helped make the tractor distinctive. The XO-121 tractor is now displayed at the Floyd County Museum in Charles City, Iowa.

Oliver Super 55
1954-1958

The Super 55 was Oliver's first utility type of tractor. It developed about 35 PTO horsepower with its 4-cylinder gasoline or diesel engines.

In the summer of 1951 Oliver started developing the specifications for a low cost utility tractor. It was to use the transmission from the model 60 and the PTO was to be controlled with the tractor's clutch. Four of these experimental tractors were assembled in June 1952. By December 1952 it was decided to upgrade the specifications to include a helical gear transmission, an independent PTO, and greater horsepower. Six experimental units of this improved configuration were built in June 1953. The pilot run production started in July 1954 and this tractor was introduced as the Super 55.

The Super 55 was Oliver's first tractor with the utility type of configuration with an adjustable front axle and the operator positioned astraddle of the transmission case. Although the hood height was just over 50 inches, the crop clearance was 20 inches. Oliver classified the Super 55 with its 3-point hitch as a 2-3 plow tractor.

The basic structure of the Super 55 included a cast engine frame which attached to the transmission case at the rear and provided the pivot point for the front axle. Mounted in the cast frame was either a gasoline or diesel engine. Both of these 4-cylinder Waukesha-Oliver engines had a displacement of 144 cubic inches, resulting from a bore and stroke of 3.50 x 3.75 inches. The valve-in-head engine had a rated speed of 2,000 rpm. The compression ratio of the gasoline engine was increased to 7.0 to 1 compared to the 6.75 to 1 used in the 66 and 77 engines. The diesel engine was a full diesel engine, since it started on diesel fuel. Both engines used the metered oil system and a cooling system with a by-pass thermostat.

The transmission provided Oliver's traditional six forward speeds and two in reverse with the two neutral position shift pattern. Speeds with the standard 10-28 (11.2-28 now) tires ranged from 1.8 to 14.2 mph. The PTO was the independent type. The belt pulley was mounted at the rear of the tractor and attached to the PTO shaft. A front PTO adapter was provided for driving a hydraulic pump or other front accessory.

The operator's steering effort was reduced with a recirculating ball mechanism. The two brake pedals for the double disc brakes were located next to each other and could be used separately for turns or together for stopping. The gauges and throttle were conveniently located on the inclined dash under the steering wheel. The Tac-Hourmeter was a new feature which provided engine speed, the travel speed for each gear, and the hours of operation.

The internal hydraulic system for the 3-point hitch could be set for draft control or depth control. When the lever was set for draft control, the top link sensed the load and the hydraulic system raised or lowered the implement to maintain a constant draft. When the lever was set for depth control, the tools stayed at a constant depth, regardless of the variation in draft.

Originally the Super 55 model was equipped with green wheels. However, any tractor shipped after January 1, 1957, was equipped with red wheels.

The performance of the Super 55 was evaluated at Nebraska in October 1954 with two tests.

Model	Test No.	Type of Test	Drawbar Hp	Belt Hp
Super 55 Gasoline	524	Corrected	30.75	35.88
Super 55 Diesel	526	Corrected	28.97	34.09

The Oliver Super 55 was equipped with a 3-point hitch and a wide variety of 3-point implements, such as this disk, were available.

Oliver Super 66, 77 & 88
1954-1958

Late in 1954 the Super 66, Super 77, and Super 88 were introduced as the replacements for the 66, 77, and 88 tractors. The new models provided more power and the Super 88 was advertised in 1955 as the most powerful row-crop tractor built. Also, Oliver discontinued the engine side panels and the Row Crop and Standard designations on the tractor. The wheels for the Super series were green instead of red, but returned to red again after January 1, 1957.

The Super 66 was built in a row-crop configuration. The Super 77 and Super 88 were available as a row-crop, standard-tread, or orchard tractor. By 1956 the Super 77 and Super 88 were also available as high clearance tractors with almost 36 inches of front axle clearance. The row-crop configurations of all three models could be equipped with a single front wheel, closely spaced dual front wheels, or an adjustable front axle.

The jointly developed and manufactured Waukesha-Oliver gasoline engines for the Super series were designed as diesel engines first, so the diesel versions used the same bore and stroke. The Super 66 moved up to a 2-3 plow rating by increasing the bore from 3.31 to 3.50 inches and thus using the same 4-cylinder engine as the Super 55. The engine for the Super 77

The Super 66 used the same 4-cylinder engine as the Super 55. A 6-cylinder version of this engine powered the Super 77.

The 6-cylinder engine for the Super 88 had an increased power output of 58 belt horsepower and a full 4-plow rating.

continued to be a 6-cylinder version of the 4-cylinder engine, so the Super 77 became a 3-4 plow tractor. The Super 88 became a full 4-plow tractor as its bore increased to 3.75 inches from 3.50. A factory-installed LP gas system was available for the Super 77 and Super 88 by 1956.

The row-crop frame for the Super series was revised to include new mounting pads for drive-in implements and front mounted weights. However, the traditional two holes for the cross pipes for mid-mounted implements also were provided.

The 6-speed transmission with its 2-position neutral shift pattern was retained which provided speeds from 2.1 to 10.5 mph for the Super 66 to 2.5 to 11.8 mph for the Super 88. The belt pulley was still located on the right side of the tractor and PTO continued to be independently controlled.

New Hydra-lectric and conventional hydraulic systems were made available for all three models. The two systems were identical, with convenient levers extending upward toward the operator from the unit, except the Hydra-lectric system featured the adjustment of the depth control collar on the remote cylinder from the tractor seat. However, if the electrical wiring was not connected to the cylinder, the Hydra-lectric system automatically reverted to manual control.

The Super series continued to be improved. A 12-volt electrical system with key starting was added for all three types of engines and a Tac-Hourmeter became standard equipment. By 1956 full-time power steering was available. Power-adjusted rear wheels were made available as special equipment. Another option was a new heavy-duty 3-point hitch which was powered with an external 4-inch hydraulic cylinder.

Both the gasoline and diesel versions were tested at Nebraska in October 1954 and May 1955, but the results were nearly identical for the two types of engines. The gasoline results were:

Model	Test No.	Type of Test	Drawbar Hp	Belt Hp
Super 66 Gasoline	541	Corrected	29.60	35.54
Super 77 Gasoline	542	Corrected	40.16	46.18
Super 88 Gasoline	525	Corrected	49.81	58.08

Oliver Super 99 & Super 99 GM

1954-1958

The Super 99 GM used a 2-cycle diesel engine to produce 83 belt horsepower and claim the title of most powerful wheel tractor built in the mid-1950s.

Two additional models, the Super 99 and the Super 99 GM, were introduced in late 1954 to make a line of six models of Oliver tractors with similar styling and sales features. The Super 99 and Super 99 GM, which replaced the 99, were the large standard-tread models of this new family and were built at South Bend Plant Number 2. The Super 99 GM was rated as a 5-6 plow tractor with 80 belt horsepower while the Super 99 was rated as a 4-5 plow tractor with 65 belt horsepower.

The Super 99 was powered with either the 6-cylinder gasoline or diesel Waukesha-Oliver engines which were introduced in 1952 for the styled 99. They shared many common parts because they were derived from the same basic engine.

In order to fit a higher horsepower engine into the frame of the Super 99, Oliver's tractor engineers turned to the General Motors 3-71 to create the Super 99 GM model. The 3-71 was a 2-cycle, 3-cylinder diesel engine with a bore and stroke of 4.25 x 5.00 inches. Since it was a 2-cycle engine, operating at the same rated speed of 1,675 rpm, its three cylinders developed the same number of power strokes as its 6-cylinder, 4-cycle counterparts. Thus it was able to develop more horsepower with its 213-cubic-inch displacement than the 302-cubic-inch, 4-cycle engine. A blower was used to force air into the cylinders during the beginning of the intake and compression stroke. The GM diesel was equipped with two air cleaners with the intakes above the hood, so this model was easily recognized by

The Super 99 was powered with either a 6-cylinder gasoline or diesel engine which provided 65 belt horsepower.

sight and its unique 2-cycle sound.

The six forward speeds of the Super 99 ranged from 2.5 to 12.8 mph with 14-34 (16.9-34 now) rear tires. The Super 99 GM was equipped with larger 15-34 (18.4-34 now) rear tires, so its six forward speeds ranged from 2.6 to 13.7 mph. The PTO was the independently controlled type and the belt pulley was located at the back of the tractor, driven by the PTO. A hydraulic system was available for the operation of a remote hydraulic cylinder with a 16-inch stroke.

Operator comfort and convenience started with the steering geometry which reduced shock by placing the front wheel kingpin inward of the front wheel, almost to the centerline of the front tire. This arrangement was combined with a recirculating ball mechanism to reduce the steering effort to that of competitive tractors with power steering. However, power steering was available to further reduce the steering effort. The steering geometry also provided an outside turning radius of only 10 feet, 1 inch.

The rubber torsion spring seat could be equipped with a spring tension back rest for additional comfort. The two brake pedals, which were connected with an equalizer pedal for use as the master brake pedal, operated double disc brakes located on the differential shaft. The instruments were located in a cluster next to the steering column and a Tac-Hourmeter was optional. Also optional was an overcenter hand clutch for those who preferred a hand clutch to a clutch pedal.

By the mid-1950s, diesel engines were the popular choice for tractors of this size and only the two diesel versions were tested at Nebraska in August and September 1955. The results were:

Model	Test No.	Type of Test	Drawbar Hp	Belt Hp
Super 99 Diesel	557	Corrected	60.90	65.01
Super 99 GM Diesel	556	Corrected	77.44	83.46

A Family of Tractors
1955

By 1955, for the first time since the early 1930s, the Oliver line of wheel-type tractors represented a family of models with similar sales features and styling. During the late 1930s and early 1940s each tractor model was designed as an individual unit, sharing very few features with the other models in the line. One or two were styled while the others were not. One model had a 6-cylinder engine while larger models had 4-cylinder engines. When 75 percent of one row-crop model was being sold with an electric starter, the next size of row-crop tractor could not be equipped with an electric starter. One model had an upholstered spring seat while another had a hammock type and others had a pan seat on a coil spring. The location of the operator's controls varied between models.

The trend toward a common design started in 1948 with the Fleetline series in which the three models shared the same styling and featured the same type of engines, a 6-speed transmission, an independent

PTO, and the same type of operator's station. However at that time, the 99 was still unstyled, had a 4-cylinder engine with a large cubic inch displacement, a 4-speed transmission, and a conventional PTO.

With the introduction of the Super series, the six models in the line represented a family. The same styling was used throughout the line from the Super 55 to the Super 99 GM. A 10 horsepower difference existed between the models. The Super 55 and Super 66 started with a 4-cylinder engine and then the Super 77 stepped up to a 6-cylinder engine with the same bore and stroke, followed by two progressively larger 6-cylinder engines. The first five models were available with gasoline or diesel engines with many common parts. Each model had a 6-speed transmission and an independent PTO. The operator's stations were generally organized in the same way and featured the rubber torsion spring seat.

The Super series of Oliver tractors was a family of models with similar styling, engines, and features from the Super 55 through the Super 99.

Oliver Super 44
1957-1958

Starting in 1947 the industry built large numbers of tractors for about six years. Since it was generally assumed the life of a tractor was about 10 years, Oliver decided there would be a large replacement market for tractors starting about 1957. One of the popular models to be replaced would be the small general purpose tractor designed for 1-row cultivation. So in 1957 they introduced a new size to the line, the Super 44, which had been planned to be built at the Battle Creek, Michigan, plant, but was actually produced at the South Bend Plant Number 2.

The Super 44 was rated as a 2-plow tractor, with 21 drawbar horsepower and 25 on the belt. It was an offset cultivation type of tractor with the engine centerline set 6.50 inches to the left of the tractor's centerline and the seat offset to the right. Crop clearance under the axles was 21.5 inches and the rear wheel tread could be adjusted from 40 to 68 inches. The rear axle housings were the drop type with the final drive gears located next to the rear wheels.

This small tractor could be equipped with three stages of hydraulic systems. The first consisted of an internal hydraulic system with a control lever for the 3-point hitch. Next was a front rockshaft and hydraulic cylin-

The first experimental Oliver offset tractor, with the engine to the left and the operator to the right, was built in 1950. The final version, the Super 44, was introduced in 1957.

der with a second lever to raise and lower the mid-mounted implements. The third stage used a third lever to operate a remote hydraulic cylinder.

The Super 44 was powered with a 4-cylinder, L-head type of Continental engine with a displacement of 140 cubic inches. The transmission provided four speeds ranging from 2.1 to 11.4 mph with the standard 9-24 (9.5-24 now) rear tires. Other options included a rubber torsion spring seat, PTO, and a rear-mounted belt pulley.

The Super 44 was not tested at the Nebraska Tractor Test Laboratory and only 775 were built in three production runs.

Oliver 550
1958-1975

Six new tractors with three digit model numbers were introduced in 1958 as the replacements for five models of the Super series. The obvious difference was the new color scheme of Meadow Green, accented with Clover White on the wheels and grill. The grill was revised to one with undivided horizontal slots and above the grill was the Oliver name in an oval frame.

The smallest of the new 1958 models was the 550 which replaced the Super 55. In late 1958 the size of the 4-cylinder gasoline and diesel engines increased from 144 to 155 cubic inches by increasing the bore .12 inches to 3.62 inches. The compression ratios were also increased.

The transmission retained the six forward speeds. The PTO was the independent type and the optional belt pulley was driven by the PTO. The internal hydraulic system for the 3-point hitch now operated as a position control system until a draft load was applied and then it automatically became a draft control system. An optional external valve controlled a remote cylinder.

Operator comfort and safety were improved by adding a safety interlock which required the clutch pedal to be depressed before the key start would engage. Power steering and power adjustable rear wheels were also made available.

The Oliver 550 was first built with a grill with horizontal slots.

For the 1963 model year the 550 changed to a checkerboard style of grill.

The 660 followed the tradition of the Super series and shared the 4-cylinder gasoline and diesel engines with the 550. These jointly developed and manufactured Waukesha-Oliver engines had a 155-cubic-inch displacement, resulting from a 3.62- x 3.75-inch bore and stroke. The compression ratio was now 7.75 to 1 for the gasoline version and 16 to 1 for the diesel. The sliding spur gear transmission provided six forward speeds and two in reverse. Travel speeds ranged from 2.4 to 11.9 mph with 9-38 (9.5-38 now) rear tires. Other rear tire sizes were the 10-38 (11.2-38 now) and the new 12.4-38 for more floatation.

Power could be transmitted with the belt pulley located on the right side of the tractor, the independent PTO, and the conventional or Hydra-electric hydraulic system. Also available was a 3-point hitch operated with an external hydraulic cylinder. Mid-mounted implements could be attached to the front and side mounting pads or with the pipe openings in the main frame.

Standard operator features included a key start for the 12-volt electrical starting system, a Tac-Hourmeter, and double disc brakes controlled by Oliver's 3-pedal system. The power-adjusted rear wheels were optional as was power steering for the single front wheel version. Serviceability was improved with an easy-to-reach grease fitting for the clutch release bearing.

The Oliver 660 was not tested at the Nebraska Tractor Testing Laboratory, but its performance would have been similar to the 550.

In 1959 Nebraska replaced the belt test with a PTO test and stopped listing "corrected horsepower." Thus "observed maximum horsepower" became the number advertised by most tractor companies. The two 550s were tested at Nebraska in May 1959 by the revised test.

Model	Test No.	Type of Test	Drawbar Hp	PTO Hp
550 Gasoline	697	Maximum	35.45	41.39
550 Diesel	698	Maximum	35.37	39.21

Oliver 660
1959-1964

The 660 was introduced for 1959, one year later than the other three digit models. It replaced the Super 66, but retained the curved grill with the divided horizontal slots used on the Super 66. However, it was painted in the new Meadow Green and Clover White colors. The 660 was described as a full 3-plow tractor with its increased horsepower. It could be equipped with closely spaced dual front wheels, a single front wheel, or an adjustable wide front axle.

The Oliver 660 was painted the new colors of Meadow Green and Clover White used for the other three digit models, but retained the styling of the Super series.

Oliver 770 & Oliver 880
1958-1967 & 1958-1963

Power was the key word Oliver used to advertise the new 770 and 880 models which were introduced in January 1958 at the Harrisburg Farm Show to replace the Super 77 and Super 88. These two models were styled and painted similar to the 550. Both new models were built in the row-crop configuration with a choice of dual front wheels, single front wheel, adjustable front axle, or a standard front axle which was non-adjustable. The 770 and 880 were available as Wheatland versions, the new name for the Standard version, and as extra high clearance units. Also the 770 was available as an orchard tractor.

Power was used to describe the new ratings of 3-4 plow for the 770 and 4-5 plow for the 880. These higher ratings were obtained by increasing the rated speed of the Waukesha-Oliver gasoline and diesel engines to 1,750 rpm. Also the compression ratio of the gasoline engine increased to 7.3 to 1, but the displacement remained at 216 cubic inches for the 770 and 265 cubic inches for the 880. An LP-gas engine also was available for both models.

Power-Booster Drive was the name of a new optional transmission package for the 770 and 880. This new unit permitted downshifting on-the-go in each of the regular speeds to obtain a 32 percent increase in pulling power with a 24 percent decrease in speed. Thus with the Power-Booster Drive, the tractor had 12-forward speeds and four in reverse. The

Power was the key word used in the introduction of the 770 and 880 early in 1958.

If a Power-Booster Drive was installed in the space previously used for the belt pulley, the 770 and 880 could be downshifted on-the-go in each gear.

Power-Booster consisted of a gear housing with three gears and two clutches and could be installed by the dealer. The Power-Booster Drive required the belt pulley to be located at the rear of the tractor and operated by the PTO drive. The 770 had a sliding spur gear transmission and the 880 was equipped with a constant mesh, helical gear transmission.

Power-Traction Hitch was a new 3-point hitch for the 770 and 880. It was designed for flexibility and convenience as it was adaptable to Category 1 or 2 sizes of pins and was equipped with spring latches at the ends of the lower links. It was powered with an external hydraulic cylinder.

Power steering and power adjustable rear wheels were two other options which could be added to the 770 and 880. The rear tire sizes continued to grow wider as a new 15.5-38 rear tire was available for both models for improved traction and floatation.

The 770 and 880 retained many of the features from the earlier Oliver models such as the independent PTO, the choice of a conventional hydraulic system or the Hydra-lectric, the seat with the rubber torsion springs, double disc brakes mounted on the differential shaft, and an equalizer pedal located between the other two brake pedals. New features included a twin dial instrument cluster, with most of the gauges and indicators grouped in one dial and the Tac-hourmeter in the other.

For 1964 the 770 was updated with a checkerboard grill, flat-top fenders with built-in lights, the tapered metal name plate on the sides of the hood, and full hydraulic power steering.

Oliver tested the 770 and 880 at Nebraska in May 1958, so they were evaluated by the earlier test procedure. The performance of the gasoline tractors were:

Model	Test No.	Type of Test	Drawbar Hp	Belt Hp
770 Gasoline	648	Corrected	45.05	51.63
880 Gasoline	647	Corrected	56.29	64.21

Oliver 950, 990 GM, & 995 GM
1958-1961

Three replaced two when the 950, 990 GM, and 995 GM Lugmatic were introduced in early 1958 as replacements for the Super 99 and the Super 99 GM. The colors and the styling changed to match the other new tractors introduced in 1958. With increases in power, the 950 moved up to a 5-6 plow rating and the 990 GM became a full 6-plow

The Oliver 950 displayed the new green and white colors instead of the traditional green body, red wheels, and yellow grill.

tractor. Production started at South Bend Plant Number 2, but was moved to the Charles City factory in mid-1958 as Oliver started consolidating their tractor manufacturing at one plant. Also the Oliver 990 GM with different sheet metal, seat, and paint was sold as the Massey Ferguson 98.

The 950 was powered with either a 6-cylinder gasoline or diesel engine which were jointly developed and manufactured by Waukesha and Oliver. The displacement of these two engines remained at 302 cubic inches, but the rated speed increased 125 rpm to 1,800 rpm. The compression ratio of the diesel version was increased to 16 to 1. The two GM models used the same GM 3-71 2-cycle engine as the Super 99 GM, but the engine speed was increased to 1,800 rpm on the 950 GM and to 2,000 rpm on the 995 GM Lugmatic.

Two types of 6-speed transmissions were available for the 950, 990, and 995. One was the standard Oliver type of transmission with one lever and a shift pattern with two neutral positions. The other one provided one lever to select one of three forward speeds and a second lever to select a high or low range. The two lever type was better suited for applications with varying draft loads which required more shifting between two gears.

The 995 GM Lugmatic used an Allison hydraulic torque converter in conjunction with one of the 6-speed transmissions. The torque converter automatically caused the drawbar pull to increase as the tractor's speed decreased without the need to downshift, thus making the tractor more convenient to drive when the tractor was operating in conditions with widely varying loads. It would enable the tractor to do more work during a period of time because time wasn't lost shifting gears and the amount of wheel slippage was reduced. However, it did not increase drawbar horsepower because the torque converter was not as efficient as a mechanical transmission.

The three 900 series models could be equipped with an independent PTO and a belt pulley which was located at the rear of the tractor, driven by the PTO. The Hydra-electric system could be used to power 3- or 4-inch remote hydraulic cylinders. A third rear tire size, 18-26 (23.1-26 now), was available along with the 14-34 and 15-34 (16.9-34 and 18.4-34 now) sizes.

The 900 series continued with the wide operator's platform with a flat deck. The fenders were revised to include extra wide extensions that reached far over the rear tires. A weatherproof cab was available which was tall enough to permit the operator to stand.

The three diesel powered models were tested at Nebraska in July 1958 and recorded the following performances:

The 995 GM Lugmatic combined the GM 3-71 2-cycle engine with a 6-speed transmission and an Allison hydraulic torque converter.

Model	Test No.	Type of Test	Drawbar Hp	Belt Hp
950 Diesel	660	Corrected	64.68	70.32
990 GM Diesel	661	Corrected	81.20	88.46
995 GM Lugmatic Diesel	662	Corrected	74.54	89.39

Oliver 440
1960 & 1962

The 440 replaced the Super 44 model for 1960, but there were only minor differences between the two models. The 440 continued to be rated as a 2-plow tractor, with 21 drawbar horsepower and 25 PTO horsepower. Production of the 440 was at the Charles City tractor factory, because South Bend Plant Number 2 was closed and sold in 1958.

The frame for the 440 was reinforced with the addition of welded angles and plates, which had started with the last Super 44s. The front wheel tread was still adjustable in 4-inch steps from 44 to 64 inches, plus an additional 71-inch setting. The rear wheel tread was also adjustable in 4-inch steps from 40 to 68 inches by changing the rims on the wheel discs.

The 440 continued to use the 4-cylinder Continental engine with a bore and stroke of 3.19 x 4.38 inches. The rated engine speed was 1,800 rpm. The four forward speeds with the optional 10-24 (11.2-24 now) rear tires were 2.2, 3.3, 4.7, and 11.8 mph.

The optional PTO was driven from the tractor's transmission, so it was not the independent type. The 3-point hitch was described as very sensitive because it used hydraulics to sense the draft instead of a mechanical system with a spring. The hydraulic system continued to be available in three versions. However, as with the Super 44, the front rockshaft could be operated with the one control lever version by using a link to connect the front rockshaft to the rockshaft which controlled the 3-point hitch.

The 440 was not tested at the Nebraska Tractor Testing Laboratory and only 700 were built, 500 in 1960 and 200 in 1962.

The Oliver 440 replaced the Super 44, but followed the pattern set by the 660 by using the new colors, but retaining the styling of the Super series.

The Oliver 500 was a lower-cost utility tractor built by David Brown Industries in England. It was available with either a 4-cylinder gasoline or diesel engine.

Oliver 500
1960-1963

The 500 represented a new era of Oliver tractors as it was the first model that was not manufactured by the company. Companies usually turned to purchased products when the estimated sales were too small to pay for the tooling costs of a new model and still have a competitive retail price. This lower-cost utility tractor with an adjustable front axle was manufactured by David Brown Industries of Meltham, England. However, it was painted Oliver colors, carried the Oliver nameplate, and had a checkerboard pattern grill. It was rated as a 2-3 plow tractor.

The 500 was powered by a 4-cylinder gasoline or diesel engine, both with a 3.50-inch bore and a 4.00-inch stroke. The 154-cubic-inch engines had overhead valves and wet sleeves, but the compression ratio of 6.25 to 1 for the gasoline version was less than the ratio used in the other Oliver models. The rated engine speed was 2,000 rpm.

The transmission with two gear shift levers provided six forward speeds and two in reverse. With the 11-28 (12.4-28 now) rear tires, the travel speeds ranged from 2.1 to 14.2 mph. A differential lock was provided to stop slippage by one rear wheel. The PTO and hydraulic system were live, but not independent. A 2-stage clutch stopped the travel of the tractor when the pedal was depressed half-way and stopped all functions when it was completely depressed. A belt pulley could be added at the rear of the tractor. The 3-point hitch was draft sensitive and an auxiliary hydraulic valve was available to control a remote cylinder.

The 500 was tested at Nebraska in March 1960 as the David Brown 850 with the following maximum observed results:

Model	Test No.	Type of Test	Drawbar Hp	Belt Hp
David Brown 850 Gas	735	Maximum	28.90	32.00
David Brown 850 Diesel	734	Maximum	31.84	33.56

Higher Horsepower
with the Oliver Models

Oliver 1800
1960-1962

During the late 1950s the trend toward fewer, but larger farms began to accelerate as Midwest farmers increased the size of their operations to decrease their cost of production. In answer to this trend, the Oliver Corporation, in the summer of 1960, introduced a larger row-crop model with more horsepower. The new 1800 was rated as a 6-plow tractor with a choice of 6-cylinder gasoline, LP-gas, or diesel engines. The row-crop version was available with dual front wheels or an adjustable front axle. The Wheatland and Ricefield versions had a nonadjustable front axle, a shorter wheelbase, and panels which enclosed the front of the operator platform.

The performance and durability of the new 1800 tractors were evaluated on the test track located at the factory in Charles City, Iowa.

The 1800 started a new trend in Oliver styling with its cast-iron grill with a checkerboard pattern and flat-top fenders with dual headlights. Steps were provided for mounting the tractor from the left side, in front of the rear wheel. A new upholstered seat with a padded back rest was combined with the rubber torsion springs for added comfort. The two brake pedals for the double disc brakes were positioned together and located on the right side of the tractor.

The new Waukesha-Oliver gasoline engine for the 1800 was the result of the knowledge learned from the XO-121 research engine and additional development work with modified Super 88 gasoline engines. The result was a 7-bearing crankshaft, a full pressure lubrication system, a new high lift camshaft, and a 8.5 to 1 compression ratio. This resulted in almost 74 observed PTO horsepower and a gasoline fuel economy record of 13.18 hp-hr/gal, the thriftiest gasoline tractor in the history of the Nebraska tests.

The Waukesha-Oliver diesel engine for the 1800 departed from Oliver's traditional approach of having the diesel and gasoline engines with the same bore and stroke. The 1800 diesel engine had a bore of 3.88 inches instead of the 3.75 inches used by the gasoline engine. However the .12-inch larger bore did not fully compensate, as the power of the diesel engine with its 16 to 1 compression ratio and 2,000 rpm rated speed was 3-4 horsepower less than the gasoline engine.

The 1800 had a constant mesh helical gear transmission with the usual six forward speeds. With the addition of Hydra-Power Drive, which permitted downshifting on-the-go, the 12 forward speeds ranged from 1.1 to 14.0 mph with 15.5-38 rear tires. The independent PTO could operate at either 540 or 1,000 rpm. The rockshaft for the 3-point hitch was now powered by integral hydraulics.

The 1800 tractor followed Oliver's concept of a balanced design between horsepower and weight. With a shipping weight of about 8,000 pounds and 70-74 PTO horsepower, the 1800 provided excellent performances with the 6-bottom Oliver 5540 semi-mounted plow in public demonstrations.

In their October 1960 tests at Nebraska, the 1800 Gasoline developed a maximum drawbar pull of 10,619 pounds and the 1800 Diesel pulled a maximum of 11,040 pounds. The observed maximum horsepower results were:

The new Oliver 1800 was a row-crop tractor for the larger Midwestern farms, providing over 70 PTO horsepower.

Model	Test No.	Type of Test	Drawbar Hp	PTO Hp
1800 Gasoline	766	Maximum	63.71	73.92
1800 Diesel	767	Maximum	62.55	70.15

(seal illustration) THE OLIVER CORPORATION · 25 YEARS OF SIX-CYLINDER POWER · BUILDING FOR YOUR FARM FUTURE

Oliver 1900
1960-1962

The trend toward larger farms was also taking place in the wheat growing areas, so Oliver introduced a larger standard-tread configuration tractor for that area in the summer of 1960. The 1900, the other half of Oliver's new power team, replaced the 950, 990, and 995 Lugmatic and was rated as an 8-plow tractor. Its styling was similar to the 1800 with a cast-iron grill with a checkerboard pattern and flat-top fenders with dual headlights. Like the 1800, the 1900 had a checkerboard stripe that extended down each side of the hood.

The largest wheel tractor in the Oliver lineup was again powered with a General Motors 2-cycle diesel engine, but this one was a 4-cylinder model. The GM 4-53 engine had a bore and stroke of 3.88 x 4.50 inches for a displacement of 53 cubic inches per cylinder and 212 cubic inches for the four cylinders. The rated speed was 2,000 rpm and the compression ratio was 17 to 1. Again the 1900 could be distinguished by its two air cleaner stacks which extended through the hood and its unique sound. A gasoline engine was not available for the 1900, indicating the popularity of diesel engines for this size of tractor by 1960.

The transmission for the 1900 was a constant mesh helical gear design with the six forward speeds ranging from 1.5 to 13.4 mph with 23.1-26 rear tires. The Hydra-Power Drive permitted downshifting on-the-go in each gear, thus providing 12 forward speeds.

The optional belt pulley attached to the PTO at the rear of the tractor. The independent PTO was available in two speeds, 540 or 1,000 rpm. The PTO lever, with a locking latch to prevent accidental

The 3-point hitch of the 1800 or 1900 enabled them to work well with the new Oliver 5540 semi-mounted plow.

engagement, was located to the left of the seat. The 1900 could be equipped with the same hydraulic system as the 1800, with the control levers located to the right of the seat.

The 1900 was equipped with a hinged door between the hood and left fender for entry to the operator platform which was enclosed in front. The upholstered seat was the same as the one provided for the 1800. Power steering was available. All the gauges, including the Tac-hourmeter, were located on the inclined dash. For safety, the gear shift had to be in neutral before the engine could be started.

The 1900 was tested at the Nebraska Tractor Testing Laboratory in October 1960 where it surpassed the maximum observed horsepower performance of the 950, 990, and 995 Lugmatic. In Test 768, the 1900 produced 82.85 observed maximum drawbar horsepower and 89.35 observed maximum PTO horsepower. The 1900 had a maximum pulling effort of 12,475 pounds.

The new Oliver 1900 was built for the larger farms in the Wheat Belt, providing 89 PTO horsepower with its 4-cylinder, 2-cycle GM diesel engine.

The Ricefield 1900 was equipped with a different style of tires and could be equipped with a 3-point hitch or this heavy-duty drawbar.

A Change in Ownership
1960

On October 31, 1960, the Oliver Corporation was purchased by the White Motor Company of Cleveland, Ohio. The purchase included only the farm equipment business with an option to purchase the crawler line, but not the factory, at a later time. The purchase did include the Oliver factories at Charles City, Iowa; South Bend, Indiana; Battle Creek, Michigan; and Shelbyville, Illinois.

White Motor manufactured heavy-duty trucks and wanted to expand into other similar industries. They emphasized the general similarity in the production and marketing of trucks and farm equipment which gave them a feeling of understanding for the opportunities and problems facing Oliver.

On November 1, 1960, Oliver started business as a wholly-owned, but separately-operated subsidiary of the White Motor Company. Samuel W. White Jr. was appointed president of the new Oliver organization. White, who was 41 years old, was not related to the founders of the White Motor Company. He had joined Oliver in 1939 at the South Bend plant and then moved to the corporate headquarters in Chicago in 1948. Later he worked in Oliver's branch house organization and then returned to Chicago to be a vice president in 1956.

Late in 1961 White Motor exercised its option and purchased the designs and tooling for only the OC-4 and OC-9 models of crawlers. The machine tools and inventory were moved to the Charles City factory and the plant's first crawler was built in June 1962.

This Oliver Shield was the company's logo from 1945 through 1960.

The new keystone type of Oliver Shield became the company's logo after being purchased by White Motor Company.

Oliver 600
1962-1963

The Oliver 600 was a big brother to the 500, being a slightly larger utility tractor. The 600 was manufactured by David Brown Industries in England and was equivalent to their 990 model. The 600 was powered with a diesel engine, which was the only type of engine available, and was rated as a 3-4 plow tractor.

The 4-cylinder engine had a displacement of 186 cubic inches, resulting from a 3.62-inch bore and a 4.50-inch stroke. The rated engine speed was 2,200 rpm and the compression ratio was 17 to 1. The manufacturer's estimated power for the tractor was 48 PTO horsepower. The twin range transmission with two gear shift levers provided six forward speeds and two in reverse. The differential lock could be engaged by a foot pedal to prevent the spinning of one rear wheel.

The 3-point hitch could be used with Category 1 or 2 size of implements and featured automatic draft control for fully-mounted 3-point hitch implements. Also, the system could operate remote hydraulic cylinders.

The live PTO could provide 540 or 1,000 rpm speeds. Again it was controlled by the 2-stage clutch pedal which stopped the forward travel, but not the PTO, when it was depressed half way. The rear-mounted belt pulley and power steering were optional.

The David Brown 990 was tested at Nebraska in June 1965, after the 600 had been discontinued by Oliver. In Test 903 it developed 45.26 maximum drawbar horsepower and 51.60 maximum PTO horsepower.

The larger Oliver 600 utility tractor was equipped with a grill with a checkerboard pattern to maintain a family appearance.

49

The Oliver 1600
was the first new
tractor model
introduced at a
"Growing O"
dealers meeting.

Oliver 1600
1962-1964

In November 1962 the Oliver Corporation introduced 23 new products for 1963 at the first of the annual "Growing O" meetings for the dealers. Heading the list was the new Oliver 1600 tractor, with an estimated 60 PTO horsepower (corrected basis) and a 4-5 plow rating. Its styling and features followed those of the 1800, except it was equipped with a tapered name plate on the hood sides.

The 1600 was available in row-crop, wheatland, and extra high clearance versions and provided a choice of gasoline, LP-gas, and diesel Waukesha-Oliver 6-cylinder engines with a rated speed of 1,900 rpm. The 3.75-inch bore of the diesel engine was .12 inches larger than the bore of the gasoline engine. The Hydra-Power Drive transmission provided 12 forward speeds and four in reverse.

The independent PTO would operate at 540 or 1,000 rpm. The integral hydraulic system featured lower link draft sensing for the 3-point hitch. Hydra-lectric control buttons could be used to adjust the depth stops on the remote hydraulic cylinders.

Operator comfort was improved with a 2-position steering wheel which could be adjusted for sitting or standing. Also, the steering column telescoped if the tractor was equipped with power steering. The throttle lever was no longer located on the steering column, moving to the right side of the dash.

In June 1963 the Oliver 1600 was tested at Nebraska and recorded the following maximum observed horsepower results:

Model	Test No.	Type of Test	Drawbar Hp	PTO Hp
1600 Gasoline	841	Maximum	48.85	56.50
1600 Diesel	840	Maximum	48.83	57.95

Revised 1800 & 1900
1962-1964

The revised 1800, which was new for 1963, was named the 1800 Series B and added the tapered name plate to its hood sides. By default the 1800 version introduced in 1960 became the Series A. Advertised at an estimated 83.5 PTO corrected maximum horsepower, the power of the gasoline engine for the 1800 Series B was increased 8 percent by enlarging the bore .12 inches and increasing the rated speed to 2,200 rpm. A power increase of 10 percent for the diesel engine was obtained by lengthening the stroke to 4.38 inches, increasing the compression ratio to 16.25 to 1, and increasing the rated speed to 2,200 rpm.

The 1800 B and 1900 B models featured increased horsepower and a new tapered name plate on each side of the hood.

The 1900 Series B with the tapered name plate on the side of the hood was also new for 1963 and thus the original 1900 became known as the 1900 Series A. With a 10 percent increase in power, the advertised horsepower of the 1900 Series B became 102 PTO horsepower, based on an estimate of the corrected power. The compression ratio of the GM 2-cycle diesel engine was increased to 21 to 1 from 17 to 1 and the rated engine speed stepped up to 2,200 rpm.

The "new for 1964" versions, 1800 C and 1900 C, included additional refinements such as full hydraulic power steering with no mechanical connection, a tilting steering wheel, a telescoping steering column, repositioned throttle lever, and an optional creeper gear.

Results of the Series B tests at Nebraska in September and November 1962 were:

Model	Test No.	Type of Test	Drawbar Hp	PTO Hp
1800 Series B Diesel	831	Maximum	67.27	77.04
1900 Series B Diesel	824	Maximum	86.68	98.54

Front-Wheel-Drive Tractors
1962-1964

As tractors continued to grow larger, Oliver's tractor engineers became concerned about the problems associated with larger two-wheel-drive tractors. These concerns included fitting wider tires between the rows, the comfort and safety of the operator at speeds above 5-6 mph, and soil compaction caused by the transfer of power by large, heavily weighted tires.

Therefore, two of the 23 "new for 1963" products Oliver announced were, in their terminology, the 1800 four-wheel-drive tractor and the 1900 four-wheel-drive tractor. Since that time the industry has come to use the term of four-wheel drive to describe tractors with equal size wheels on two powered axles and the term of front-wheel assist or front-wheel drive to describe the type of powered front axle introduced by Oliver.

The front-wheel drive increased the drawbar pull 20 to 40 percent in difficult traction conditions, provided better flotation in loose or muddy ground, provided better control and handling on hillsides, and improved turning in soft conditions.

This new front-wheel drive was a mechanical type with the power being transmitted from the front of the transmission to a transfer drive case and

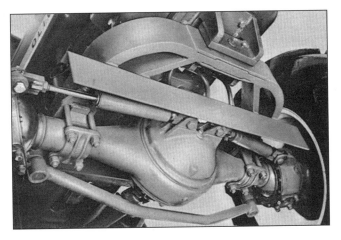

then with a drive shaft to the differential in the front axle. The transfer case attached to the front of the transmission and extended downward to minimize the angles in the drive shaft. It included a sliding collar with a small lever under the tractor's dash to disengage the drive when traveling at transport speeds or when the drawbar load was small. The front axle was equipped with constant velocity universal joints to smoothly transmit the power. Planetary gears were included in the wheel hubs for the final reduction.

This view of the front-wheel drive reveals the heavy-duty construction of the mechanically powered front axle and the steering cylinders.

The two power steering cylinders were located in front of the axle and a bumper was provided to protect them from obstructions. Clearance was 13.5 to 14 inches under the front axle and the front axle could oscillate within a 30 degree range. The turning radius was less than 14 feet.

The size of front wheel had to be matched with the rear wheel, so the customer originally had two choices. The 12.4-24 front tires were matched with 23.1-26 rear tires or the front had to be equipped with 13.6-24 tires when 18.4-34 tires were used on the rear. By 1964 there were five combinations for the 1800 and seven for the 1900.

By 1964 the front-wheel drive was made available for the 1600, making three models which Oliver described as four-wheel-drive tractors. The 1600 was available with seven combinations of front and rear tires.

The 1800 and 1900 were tested at Nebraska in December 1962 and September 1963. Since the test track had a concrete surface, the front-wheel drive did not provide an advantage in drawbar power. However, the 1900 did surpass the 100-horsepower threshold in its PTO test. The 1600 with front-wheel drive was not tested at Nebraska.

Sam White, president of Oliver, had just completed his test drive of the new front-wheel drive which was introduced in 1962 for the 1800 and 1900 models.

Model	Test No.	Type of Test	Drawbar Hp	PTO Hp
1800 B Dsl. w/ fwd	832	Maximum	64.04	76.97
1900 B Dsl. w/ fwd	847	Maximum	90.16	100.62

Oliver 1650 & 1850 and Oliver 1950
1964-1969 and 1964-1967

Three new models with exclusive factory certified horsepower were introduced as "new for 1965" at the 1964 "Growing O" dealer meetings. Manufacturing tolerances cause a variation between individual tractors in the amount of power they will produce, but factory certified horsepower meant every tractor was certified to deliver no less than its rated horsepower. The 1650 was certified to produce 66 PTO horsepower, the 1850 at 92 PTO horsepower, and the 1950 at 105 PTO horsepower. All ratings closely matched the maximum power tests at Nebraska. The new models retained the flat-top fenders, the tapered nameplate on the side of the hood, and the familiar white cast-iron grill with the checkerboard pattern.

Another popular addition was the row-crop version of the 1950 which made it the most powerful row-crop tractor on the market. It was available with dual front wheels or an adjustable front axle. The 1950 also was available in wheatland, ricefield, or front-wheel-drive versions. The 1850 could be purchased in the same five versions as the 1950 plus a high clearance version. The 1650 was built in the same five versions as the other two models plus a row-crop with a single front wheel and a high clearance version.

The Oliver 1650 was rated at 66 PTO horsepower and every 1650 produced was factory certified to produce no less than that amount.

All three models featured a new deluxe seat with a steel torsion suspension and an oil-actuated shock absorber, mounted on an inclined slide rail to better match the seat position with the length of the operator's legs. The seat and backrest were upholstered cushions as was the optional upper back rest. Also the steering wheel now had three positions plus the telescoping steering column to better adjust its position for the operator.

The power of the 1650 and 1850 was increased by moving each version to the next size of Waukesha-Oliver engine and adding a new 354-cubic-inch (initially described as a 352) Perkins diesel engine as shown in the table:

The 1950 was available with either the closely spaced front wheels or an adjustable front axle, making it the industry's most powerful row-crop tractor.

Displacement (cubic inches)	Bore (inches)	Stroke (inches)	Tractor Model	Tractor Model
248	3.62	4.00	1600 Gas	
265	3.75	4.00	1600 Dsl.	1650 Gas
283	3.88	4.00	1800 C Gas	1650 Dsl.
310	3.88	4.38	1800 C Dsl.	1850 Gas
354	3.88	5.00		1850 Dsl.

The rated engine speeds were also increased to provide more power. The LP-gas engines for the 1650 and 1850 had the same displacement as the gasoline engines. The engines were now equipped with an alternator and a new dry air cleaner.

The standard transmission provided six forward speeds and the optional Hydra-Power Drive permitted each gear to be downshifted on-the-go for a total of 12 forward speeds. In late 1967 a new Hydraul-Shift for the 1650 and 1850 provided on-the-go shifting to either a faster or slower speed in each gear for a total of 18 forward speeds. A new optional PTO permitted switching between 540 or 1,000 rpm.

The Nebraska Tractor Tests for these 50 series tractors were finished in November 1964, just before the track closed for the winter. The results of the diesel powered tests were:

Model	Test No.	Type of Test	Drawbar Hp	PTO Hp
1650 Diesel	873	Maximum	57.82	66.28
1850 Diesel	870	Maximum	81.76	92.94
1950 GM Diesel	871	Maximum	99.27	105.79

Oliver 1250
1965-1969

The Oliver 1250 tractor, a new smaller model for the utility tractor market which filled the space left by the discontinued 500 model, was introduced as "new for 1966" at the 1965 "Growing O" dealer meetings. The 1250, with a 4-cylinder engine, was manufactured by Fiat in Italy and was certified by Oliver to produce 38.5 PTO horsepower with the diesel engine and 35 with the gasoline engine.

The Fiat diesel engine's displacement was 138 cubic inches, resulting from a 3.31- x 4.00-inch bore and stroke. The Fiat gasoline engine used a 3.25- x 3.50-inch bore and stroke for a 116-cubic-inch displacement. The rated engine speed was 2,500 rpm and the compression ratios were 7.5 to 1 for the gasoline and 21.5 to 1 for the diesel engine. A 24-volt electrical system was standard with the two 12-volt batteries located between the grill and radiator for easy servicing.

The transmission for the 1250 was similar to the other Oliver models with six forward speeds which were selected

The Oliver 1250 had a checkerboard type of grill with a different pattern, but it did help tie the 1250 to the other models in the line.

with one gear shift lever. The travel speeds ranged from 1.3 to 15.6 mph with 13.6-28 rear tires. A differential lock was provided to stop one rear wheel from spinning. Operator comfort was provided with a padded seat, an inclined dash with easy-to-read gauges, and an exhaust system which was routed under the left rear axle.

The PTO was the live type, being controlled by the 2-position clutch pedal. Also, it could be set to be a ground speed PTO by moving the PTO lever forward. The Category 1 size of 3-point hitch could be set for either draft or position control. A control valve for single- or double-acting remote hydraulic cylinders was standard.

The Oliver 1250 and the corresponding Fiat 415 were not tested at the Nebraska Tractor Testing Laboratory.

Oliver 1550
1965-1969

The 1550 was the second new tractor introduced at the 1965 "Growing O" dealer meetings. Oliver's exclusive certified horsepower rating for the 1550 was 53 PTO horsepower for the gasoline and diesel powered versions and 51 PTO horsepower for the LP-gas version.

The 1550 row-crop was available with dual front wheels, single front wheel, an adjustable front axle, or a high-clearance configuration. A utility version with a lower clearance adjustable front axle and smaller diameter rear tires and a wheatland version with a solid front axle were also available. Both the 6-cylinder gasoline and diesel engines had a 232-cubic-inch displacement, but produced the same horsepower because the diesel compression ratio was maintained at 16.5 to 1, and the gasoline compression ratio was lowered to 8.0 to 1.

A 6-speed spur gear transmission was standard, but the Hydra-Power Drive was also available. The independent PTO was available as 540 rpm, 1,000 rpm, or with both speeds. The hydraulic system for the row-crop and utility versions included the 3-point hitch and two remote hydraulic cylinders.

A pan seat with a rubber torsion spring was standard for the row-crop and utility

The 1550 matched the style of the 1650, 1850, and 1950. Eventually it replaced the model 770.

versions, but the deluxe seat with the steel torsion suspension was standard for the wheatland version and optional for the others.

The two 1550 versions were tested at Nebraska in June 1966 with the following results:

Model	Test No.	Type of Test	Drawbar Hp	PTO Hp
1550 Gasoline	944	Maximum	46.20	53.34
1550 Diesel	943	Maximum	45.77	53.50

Optional Equipment
New for 1965 & 1966

Another industry first for Oliver was the introduction of Goodyear Terra Tires in July 1965 for the 1850 and 1950 tractors with the front-wheel drive. The 48-inch wide front tires and the 66-inch wide rear tires provided excellent flotation and enabled wheel tractors to do jobs which previously could be performed only by crawler tractors.

The hydraulic-powered front-wheel drive for the 1650, 1850, and 1950 row-crop tractors was a new product for 1966. With this adjustable front

The new cab with the folding doors was designed to fit between the optional fender fuel tanks.

axle, the row-crop clearance was 26 inches and the front wheel tread could be adjusted from 62 to 88 inches. A hydraulic pump was located in a housing on the front of the tractor and each front wheel was equipped with a hydraulic motor. At the maximum setting, the hydraulic drive produced 10 to 12 horsepower at each front wheel.

Dual rear tires became a popular option as tractors increased in weight and power.

To improve operator comfort, Oliver started providing field or factory installed cabs for the 1550, 1650, 1850, and 1950 models. The cab featured a folding door, tinted glass, and a filtered air intake. Optional equipment included a heavy-duty heater and a pressurizing fan to prevent dust seepage.

Other new optional equipment included dual rear wheels for the 1850 and 1950 models. A new wider 18.4-38 rear tire could be ordered and a new 11.00-16 front tire became available for the adjustable front axle. Another option was the auxiliary fender tanks for the 1650, 1850, and 1950 models. Each fender held 39 gallons, permitting long runs between refills. These replaced the regular fenders and were equipped with the same lights.

The hydraulic-powered front axle provided clearance for row crops and could be adjusted to fit the row spacing.

This Oliver tractor with a front-wheel drive is equipped with Goodyear Terra Tires.

Oliver 1750
1966-1969

The 1966 "Growing O" dealer meeting was held in Charles City, so the dealers toured the factory and test track and were introduced to the new 1750 tractor. This "new for 1967" model with 80 certified PTO horsepower was rated as a 5-6 plow tractor. Oliver now had a line of six models from 38.5 to 105 PTO horsepower, with about 13 horsepower between models.

The 1750 was available as a wheatland, a ricefield, or a row-crop tractor with a choice of four fronts: dual front wheels, a regular tread adjustable front axle, a narrow tread adjustable front axle, and the under-mounted utility type of front axle. Also the 1750 could be equipped with the either the mechanical or the hydraulic front-wheel drive.

The Waukesha-Oliver 6-cylinder, 283-cubic-inch gasoline and 310-cubic-inch diesel engines were the same size as those used by the 1800 Series B and C models, but the rated speed was increased to 2,400 rpm. The constant mesh helical gear transmission with the optional Hydra-Power Drive provided 12 forward speeds.

The 1750 shared many of the features of the 1650 and 1850 such as the three types of independent PTO drive and the internal hydraulic system for the 3-point hitch. The operator's station included the Tilt-O-Scope steering column and the adjustable upholstered seat. The new Oliver Continental cab provided more room inside and an optional air conditioning system.

The performance of the two Oliver 1750 tractors at Nebraska in June 1967 was:

Model	Test No.	Type of Test	Drawbar Hp	PTO Hp
1750 Gasoline	961	Maximum	68.92	80.31
1750 Diesel	962	Maximum	68.37	80.05

The Oliver 1750 filled the power gap between the 66-horsepower 1650 and the 92-horsepower 1850.

Oliver 1450
1967-1969

The Oliver 1450 was introduced at the 1967 "Growing O" dealer meetings as "new for 1968." It was an additional model of a utility type of tractor with 55 certified PTO horsepower and was manufactured by Fiat in Italy, corresponding to their model 615. The appearance and styling of the 1450 was the same as the 1250.

The 1450 was powered with a 4-cylinder Fiat diesel engine with a rated engine speed of 1,900 rpm. Its displacement was 268 cubic inches, resulting from a 4.25-inch bore and a 4.75-inch stroke. This diesel engine had a compression ratio of 15.5 to 1 as compared to the 21.5 to 1 used in the engine for the 1250.

The transmission provided seven forward speeds ranging from 1.3 to 14.5 mph with 14.9-30 rear tires. An optional Ampli-couple drive reduced the speed in each gear by 33 percent and provided 14 forward speeds and 4 in reverse.

The 540 rpm PTO was the live type, not independent, and was controlled with the 2-stage main clutch pedal. The 3-point hitch was the Category 2 size and provided draft and position control. A control valve for remote hydraulic cylinders was available. The 1450 also was equipped with a foot-operated accelerator pedal and a hand-parking lever.

Optional equipment included power steering, downswept exhaust, power adjusted rear wheels, and a rear-mounted belt pulley.

The Oliver 1450 was not tested at the Nebraska Laboratory.

With a low profile and the optional front-wheel drive, the Oliver 1450 made an excellent tractor for front loader work.

Oliver 1950-T
1967-1969

The new 1950-T featured a turbocharged diesel engine and the new Over/Under Hydraul-Shift transmission.

The Oliver 1950-T with 105 factory certified PTO horsepower was the other new tractor introduced at the 1967 "Growing O" meetings. Rated as a 7-8 plow tractor, the 1950-T was Oliver's first factory turbocharged model and it was the first equipped with the new Over/Under Hydraul-Shift transmission. The 1950-T followed the traditional Oliver styling of the 1960s and replaced the 1950 with its GM 2-cycle engine.

Like the 1750, the 1950-T was available as wheatland and ricefield versions with the fixed tread front axle and as a row-crop version with a choice of dual front wheels or three types of adjustable front axles. Also the 1950-T could be fitted with either the mechanical or hydraulic front-wheel drive.

The diesel engine for the 1950-T was a turbocharged version of the Waukesha-Oliver 310-cubic-inch engine used by the 1750 with the same rated engine speed of 2,400 rpm. The turbocharger increased the engine's power by forcing more air into the combustion chambers.

The new Over/Under Hydraul-Shift transmission took on-the-go shifting one step further with a speed increase and decrease for

each of the regular gears, thus providing 18 forward speeds and 6 in reverse. Compared to the direct speed, shifting to overdrive provided a 20-percent speed increase and a 20-percent decrease in pull and the underdrive provided the opposite.

The 1950-T offered the same choice of PTO drives and hydraulic systems as the 1750 and 1850, except the 3-point hitch was either Category 2 or the new Category 3. Cabs, fender fuel tanks, and dual rear wheels were available.

Nebraska Test 969 of November 1967 measured the maximum power of the 1950-T which was 93.47 horsepower on the drawbar and 105.24 PTO horsepower. The fuel efficiency of 16.20 hp-hr/gal during the PTO test was the first time an Oliver tractor had exceeded 16.00 hp-hr/gal.

The turbocharger for the 1950-T was mounted above the 310-cubic-inch diesel engine.

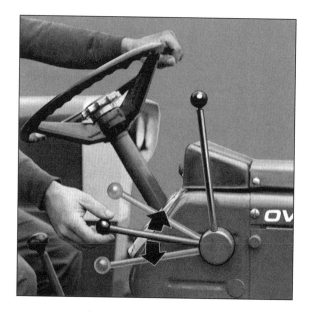

The new Over/Under Hydraul-Shift was controlled with a lever on the right side of the dash.

Oliver 2050 & 2150
1968-1969

Two additional models, the new 2050 and 2150 tractors, represented a new level of tractor power for Oliver. Factory certified PTO horsepower was 118 for the 2050 and 131 for the turbocharged 2150. Except for the engine and the size of the clutch, the two models were identical. The two-wheel drive versions included the row-crop, ricefield, and wheatland. All were equipped with a heavy duty adjustable front axle and a planetary drive at the end of the rear axles. The front-wheel drive version had the mechanical front-wheel drive and regular rear axles, because only two-thirds of the engine power was applied to the rear axles.

The new 478-cubic-inch engine was a White-Hercules 6-cylinder diesel power plant with a bore and stroke of 4.56 x 4.88 inches. The rated engine speed was 2,400 rpm and the compression ratio was 18.0 to 1. The engines also featured seven main bearings and aluminum pistons.

The helical gear transmission provided the regular Oliver six forward speeds and two in reverse. Adding the Over/Under Hydraul-Shift tripled the number of speeds by providing an overdrive speed, a direct speed, and an underdrive speed with on-the-go shifting in each of the regular gears. Due to the higher horsepower, only the 1,000 rpm PTO was provided.

The optional 3-point hitch featured a 6,000-pound lift for Category 3 implements by using two 3- x 8-inch external hydraulic cylinders. The system also provided outlets for two remote hydraulic cylinders. A hydraulic system with two,

The 2150 was the turbocharged version of the pair and had a clutch diameter of 14 inches.

The 2050 was naturally aspirated and was equipped with a 13-inch diameter clutch.

three, or four valves for remote hydraulic cylinders was also available.

Standard equipment included triple disc brakes, the three-position Tilt-O-Scope power steering, and the upholstered seat on the inclined rails. The fender fuel tanks were standard for the wheatland and ricefield versions and optional for the row-crop and front-wheel-drive versions. Other options included three versions of a cab and dual rear wheels.

The 2050 and 2150 were tested at Nebraska in October 1968 with the following results:

Model	Test No.	Type of Test	Drawbar Hp	PTO Hp
2050 Diesel	987	Maximum	104.52	118.78
2150 Diesel	986	Maximum	114.63	131.48

Other Corporate Changes
1963-1969

In 1962 the White Motor Company purchased Cockshutt Farm Equipment of Brantford, Ontario, and made Cockshutt a subsidiary of the Oliver Corporation. The marketing efforts in Canada of the two companies were soon merged and the Oliver combine line that was built in Battle Creek, Michigan, was replaced by combines built in Brantford. Then in 1963 White Motor Company purchased Minneapolis-Moline and operated it as a subsidiary of White Motor.

Next White Motor and Cummins Engine Company tried to consolidate into a new company, but this was not approved by the Justice Department. So in 1966 White Motor, which had changed its name from Company to Corporation, purchased the Hercules Engine Division of the Hupp Corporation.

Late in 1969 the White Motor Corporation organized the White Farm Equipment Company as a new wholly-owned subsidiary. The new White Farm Equipment organization consolidated the Oliver and Minneapolis-Moline subsidiaries and was the beginning of combining the two companies. Samuel W. White Jr. was named president of the new group.

After the 1969 corporate changes, the brand name became White Oliver for 1970. The White Oliver 1255 utility tractor was built by Fiat in Italy.

Oliver 1250-A & White Oliver 1255
1969-1971

The White Oliver 1255 utility tractor was first introduced as the Oliver 1250-A, which replaced the 1250, but became the 1255 when the other 55 series models were introduced in the autumn of 1969. The new model was equivalent to the Fiat 450 and retained the 38.5 certified horsepower rating. Versions included the regular utility type with an adjustable front axle, one with a mechanical front-wheel drive, and the narrow 1255 Vineyard.

The 1250-A and 1255 were powered with a 3-cylinder, 142.8-cubic-inch Fiat diesel engine instead of the 4-cylinder, 138-cubic-inch engine used in the 1250. The rated engine speed continued to be 2,400 rpm. The electrical system was now 12-volts and equipped with an alternator. The 6-speed transmission for the 1255 was shifted with a single lever and provided speeds from 1.4 to 14.5 with 12.4-28 rear tires. Optional creeper gears provided additional speeds of 0.4, 0.8, and 1.3 mph.

The PTO could be set for 540 rpm or as a ground speed PTO. The 540 rpm setting was a live PTO which was controlled by the 2-stage main clutch pedal. The 3-point hitch was adjustable for Category 1 or 2 implements and an external control valve was available for remote hydraulic cylinders.

The operator controls included a differential lock to stop one rear wheel from spinning, a foot accelerator, and a hand parking lever for the band type brakes.

The 1250-A and the 1255 were not tested at Nebraska.

White Oliver 1355
1969-1971

The Oliver 1450 was replaced by the White Oliver 1355 with 51 certified PTO horsepower. This utility-type tractor, which corresponded to the Fiat 550, could be equipped with a regular adjustable front axle, a high-clearance front axle, or a front-wheel drive. Also it was available as an orchard version. The styling of both the 1255 and 1355 was tied to the other models in the White Oliver line with a white grill with a checkerboard pattern.

The Fiat engine for the 1355 was a 4-cylinder version of the 3-cylinder diesel engine used by the 1255, so it had a displacement of 190.4 cubic inches. The engine in the 1355 included a dynamic balancer, two balanced weights running in opposite directions at twice the engine speed, to eliminate the vibrations found in most 4-cylinder, in-line engines.

The dual range transmission for the 1355 provided eight forward speeds and two in reverse. With 14.9-30 rear tires, the forward speeds ranged from 1.5 to 15.0 mph and the optional creeper gears added four more speeds ranging from 0.4 to 1.4 mph. The 540 rpm PTO for the 1355 was the independent type with its own clutch lever. It could also be set to provide a ground speed PTO in which the PTO rotated in a fixed ratio to the revolutions of the tractor rear wheels.

Both the 1255 and 1355 provided the same hydraulic system and 3-point hitch. The padded seat used a parallelogram suspension system for operator comfort. Power steering and power adjustable rear wheels were optional for both the 1255 and 1355.

The 1355 was not tested at the Nebraska Tractor Testing Laboratory.

A larger utility tractor was the White Oliver 1355 which was built by Fiat and had a 4-cylinder version of the engine used in the 1255.

White Oliver 1555 & 1655
1969-1975

The dealer introduction meeting for the new line of White Oliver tractors was held at Torrance, California, in November 1969. The new White Oliver models retained the characteristic styling of the previous Oliver models with the white cast-iron grill, tapered nameplate on the sides of the hood, and the flat-top fenders. However, for the 55 series the headlights were mounted in the top of the grill plus additional ones could be mounted in the fenders. Two of the new models, the 1555 and 1655, replaced the 1550 and 1650. Both were available as wheatland or ricefield versions with a fixed tread front axle and as a row-crop with dual front wheels or adjustable front axles. Also a mechanical front-wheel-drive version of the 1655 was available.

The 1555 retained the 53 certified PTO horsepower rating and the 1655 stepped up four horsepower to 70 certified PTO horsepower. Both models were available with 6-cylinder Waukesha-Oliver gasoline and diesel engines. The two engines for the 1555 had the same 232-cubic-inch displacement with a bore and stroke of 3.62 x 3.75 inches. The gasoline engine for the 1655 had a displacement of 265 cubic inches resulting from a 3.75- x 4.00-inch bore and stroke. The diesel engine for the 1655 moved up one size to 283 cubic inches, with a larger 3.88-inch bore and the same

The White Oliver 1555 continued with the 53 PTO horsepower rating and the optional Hydra-Power Drive with an underdrive for each gear.

4.00-inch stroke. All four engines were rated at 2,200 rpm. The 1555 diesel engine had a compression ratio of 16.5 to 1 because it was the same size as its gasoline counterpart and the diesel engine for the 1655 had a compression ratio of 16 to 1 because it was larger than the gasoline engine for the 1655.

The spur gear transmission for the 1555 and the helical gear transmission for the 1655 provided six forward speeds and two in reverse. Hydra-Power Drive, which was optional for the 1555, provided on-the-go shifting to an underdrive for each direct gear for a total of 12 forward speeds. The 1655 could be equipped with the Over/Under Hydraul-Shift which provided on-the-go shifting to either an overdrive or underdrive speed from the direct drive speed for a total of 18 forward speeds.

The independent PTO could be 540 rpm, 1,000 rpm, or the combination unit which provided both speeds. The 3-point hitch was Category 2, but adjustable to Category 1. The proven hydraulic system did not change with a choice of 3-point hitch plus manually-set depth stops on the remote cylinders, 3-point hitch plus Hydra-lectric to set the depth stops on the remote cylinders, or a remote cylinder system with two, three, or four stack valves.

The Tilt-O-Scope power steering for the 1555 and 1655 was improved and made more precise. The upholstered seat could be adjusted to match the operator's weight. Cabs were available as was a protective roll bar with a canopy and seat belt. Power adjustable rear wheels were optional and fender fuel tanks could be added to the 1655.

The 1555 used the Nebraska tests for the 1550 and the 1655 was tested in May 1970 with the following results:

The White Oliver 1655 stepped up to 70 PTO horsepower and was equipped with a helical gear transmission. The Over/Under Hydraul-Shift was optional for the 1655.

Model	Test No.	Type of Test	Drawbar Hp	Belt Hp
White Oliver 1555 Diesel	943	Maximum	45.77	53.50
White Oliver 1655 Diesel	1041	Maximum	61.90	70.57

White Oliver 1755, 1855, & 1955
1970-1975, 1969-1975, & 1970-1974

The 1755, 1855, and 1955 were three other new models introduced in November 1969 and replaced the 1750, 1850, and 1950-T. The certified PTO horsepower ratings were 86 for the 1755 Gasoline or Diesel, 92 for the 1855 Gasoline, 98 for the 1855 Diesel, and 108 for the 1955 Diesel. These three models maintained the new family appearance with the headlights mounted in the top of the grill. Configuration versions included the row-crop with dual front wheels or three styles of adjustable front axles, the mechanically powered front-wheel-drive version, and the wheatland and ricefield versions with the fixed tread front axle.

With the increasing popularity of tractor cabs, new features were added to provide more comfort for the operator. The platform was cushioned by rubber mounts and raised to reduce the amount of heat transferred to it. The instrument panel was mounted on a rubber seal and a rubber boot placed around the steering column to keep out dust. The Tilt-O-Scope steering wheel had more positions and improved power steering. The brakes were powered with hydraulics and the PTO clutch was engaged hydraulically, permitting gradual starts.

Factory-installed cabs, such as this one mounted on a White Oliver 1855, were becoming more popular.

The 6-cylinder diesel engines for the 1755, 1855, and 1955 illustrated a practice which became very common in farm tractors. All three had the same 310-cubic-inch displacement, with a 3.88- x 4.38-inch bore and stroke. To obtain the differences in horsepower, the engine used in the 1755 was naturally aspirated, the one for the 1855 was lightly turbocharged, and the 1955 was turbocharged.

The gasoline engine for the 1755 remained at the 283-cubic-inch size used in the 1750 and the 1855 was powered with the same basic 310-cubic-inch gasoline engine as the 1850. All the engines continued to be jointly developed and manufactured by Waukesha and White Oliver.

This White Oliver 1755 shows the White name added to the side of the tractor and the optional roll bar and canopy.

The operator's station was designed to improve the comfort of the operator and included the Tilt-O-Scope steering wheel, improved power steering, and hydraulic brakes.

The standard transmission continued to be the helical gear transmission with six forward and two reverse speeds. The Over/Under Hydraul-Shift was the optional transmission with on-the-go shifting and provided three speeds in each gear. The resulting 18 forward speeds ranged from 1.3 to 17.2 mph for the 1755 and 1855 with 18.4-34 rear tires and 1.5 to 17.2 mph for the 1955 with 23.1-34 rear tires.

A new closed center hydraulic system was featured on the 1755, 1855, and 1955 to power the 3-point hitch, remote cylinders, steering, brakes, and PTO clutch. The new system provided constant pressure with variable oil flow and provided faster cycling times and more efficiency for multiple circuits. The regular 3-point hitch was adjustable for Category 1 or 2 implements and was standard on the 1755 and 1855. The heavy-duty 3-point hitch lifted 6,000 pounds and was built for Category 2 or 3 implements. It was standard on the 1955 and optional for the 1755 and 1855. The PTO drive continued to be available as 540 rpm, 1,000 rpm, or a combination unit.

Optional equipment included a factory-installed cab, roll bar with canopy and seat belt, power adjustable rear wheels, dual rear wheels, and fender fuel tanks.

Power levels of the three new models when tested at Nebraska in May and October 1970 were:

Model	Test No.	Type of Test	Drawbar Hp	PTO Hp
White Oliver 1755 Diesel	1057	Maximum	76.38	86.93
White Oliver 1855 Diesel	1040	Maximum	84.30	98.60
White Oliver 1955 Diesel	1055	Maximum	92.85	108.16

Other popular options were dual rear tires and the fender fuel tanks as shown on this White Oliver 1955.

The largest model in the White Oliver line was the 2455 articulated, four-wheel-drive tractor with 139 engine horsepower.

White Oliver 2455
1969-1970

The White Oliver 2455, a new four-wheel-drive articulated steering model with four equally sized wheels, was the largest White Oliver tractor introduced to the dealers in November 1969. It was built by Minneapolis-Moline and was the first example of a shared tractor model within the new corporate organization.

The two-piece tractor frame was hinged and the tractor was steered by controlling the angle between the two frame members. When a drawbar load was applied, the resulting weight transfer equalized the load on both axles for maximum traction. The wheel tread was adjustable.

The 2455 was equipped with a diesel engine developing 139 engine horsepower. It was a 504-cubic-inch, 6-cylinder Minneapolis-Moline engine with a 4.62-inch bore and a 5.00-inch stroke. The rated engine speed was 1,800 rpm.

A 5-speed transmission was connected to a 2-speed transfer case to provide 10 forward speeds. Six of the 10 speeds were in the prime working range of 2 to 6.5 mph. Two sets of hydraulic outlets were provided for remote cylinders.

The operator's station was an open platform located on the front frame unit. Steps were provided on the back side of both front fenders for climbing to the platform. The steering wheel operated a hydrostatic steering system which in turn operated the two hydraulic cylinders positioned on each side of the hinge between the two frame units.

The White Oliver 2455 was not tested at Nebraska.

Oliver 1865, 2055, & 2155
1971

The Oliver 2055 was the Minneapolis-Moline G1050 painted in the Oliver colors. Its MM engine produced 110 PTO horsepower.

For 1971 Oliver added three models with the Oliver name and colors which were Minneapolis-Moline tractors, built in the MM factory. These new models included the 1865 model at 97 PTO horsepower, the 2055 with 110 PTO horsepower, and the 2155 model introduced at an estimated 135 PTO horsepower, but later rated at 141 PTO horsepower with its diesel engine.

The Oliver 1865 was based on the Minneapolis-Moline G950 and could be equipped with either a diesel or LP-gas 6-cylinder engine. The diesel engine had a bore and stroke of 4.38 x 5.00 inches with a displacement of 451 cubic inches. The 425-cubic-inch LP-gas engine was slightly smaller with a 4.25- x 5.00-inch bore and stroke. The rated engine speed was 1,800 rpm.

The Oliver 2055, based on the Minneapolis-Moline G1050, was available with an adjustable or a fixed tread front axle. It used the same 504-cubic-inch displacement for both the diesel and LP-gas 6-cylinder engines, with a 4.62- x 5.00-inch bore and stroke. Both engines were rated at 1,800 rpm and the diesel engine was naturally aspirated.

The standard transmission for the 1865 and 2055 was the 2-speed Ampli-Torc with 10 forward speeds. The optional 3-speed Ampli-Torc increased the number of forward speeds to 15. With 18.4-38 rear tires

these speeds ranged from 1.8 to 19.1 mph with the 3-speed Ampli-Torc.

The Oliver 2155, which was the Minneapolis-Moline G1350, featured the biggest diesel power plant in a two-wheel-drive tractor. With a rated speed of 2,200 rpm, this naturally aspirated, 585-cubic-inch, 6-cylinder engine had a 4.75- x 5.50-inch bore and stroke and produced 141 PTO horsepower. The LP-gas engine was a smaller 504-cubic-inch size with a 4.62-inch bore and a 5.00-inch stroke. The LP-gas engine produced 135 PTO horsepower.

The only transmission available for the 2155 was the 2-speed Ampli-Torc which provided 10 forward speeds and 2 in reverse. To reduce the load in the rear axles, the 2155 was equipped with planetary gears at the outer ends of the axles. This model could be equipped with an adjustable or a fixed tread front axle.

For all three models the independent PTO drive could be a single speed of 1,000 rpm only or a dual speed with both 540 and 1,000 rpm. A closed center hydraulic system operated the 3-point hitch which was compatible with Category 2 or 3 implements. An optional open center hydraulic system provided two or three valves for controlling remote hydraulic cylinders.

For the comfort of the operator, these tractors featured a deluxe posture-adjustable seat, convenient console controls, hydrostatic power steering, and an open, unobstructed platform. A spacious cab was available and it could be equipped with a heater, air conditioner, and radio.

The Oliver 1865 used the June 1968 Nebraska tests for the MM G900 and G950. The Oliver 2055 was tested in November 1966 as the MM G1000 and MM G1050. The Oliver 2155 and its MM counterpart were tested in June 1971 at Nebraska. The performance of the diesel powered models were:

For 1971 the Minneapolis-Moline G1350 was also marketed as the Oliver 2155. Its 585-cubic-inch diesel engine was rated at 141 PTO horsepower.

Model	Test No.	Type of Test	Drawbar Hp	PTO Hp
Oliver 1865 Diesel	978	Maximum	88.09	97.78
Oliver 2055 Diesel	953	Maximum	102.32	110.78
Oliver 2155 Diesel	1069	Maximum	125.29	141.44

White Farm Equipment Company sold a four-wheel-drive tractor with MM engines as the Oliver 2655 and the MM A4T-1600.

Oliver 2655
1971-1972

Manufactured in 1971 and 1972 and sold from 1971 through 1973, the Oliver 2655 four-wheel-drive, articulated frame tractor was the largest model in the Oliver line. It was rated at 143 PTO horsepower with the diesel engine and 135 PTO horsepower with the LP-gas engine. It was built by Minneapolis-Moline, but responsibility moved to Charles City after the MM factory was closed in 1972. The same tractor was also sold as the Minneapolis-Moline A4T-1600.

The 2655 utilized a two-piece frame with the front frame moving 44 degrees to the left or right for steering. The rear axle was mounted solidly to the rear frame, but the front axle was able to oscillate 15 degrees either way within the front frame. The wheel tread was adjustable from 76 to 96 inches to match row spacings.

The 6-cylinder MM diesel engine had a 4.75- x 5.50-inch bore and stroke for a displacement of 585 cubic inches. The MM LP-gas engine was a smaller 504 cubic inches with a 4.62- x 5.00-inch bore and stroke. The rated engine speed was 2,200 rpm for both engines.

The 5-speed transmission was combined with a 2-speed transfer case to provide 10 forward speeds and 2 in reverse. With 18.4-34 tires the travel speeds ranged from 2.1 to 11.4 mph in the low range and 4.0 to 22.0 mph in the high range. The independent PTO had a speed of 1,000 rpm.

An open center hydraulic system which provided two or three valves for the operation of remote cylinders was standard equipment. A closed center hydraulic system with a 3-point hitch for Category 2 or 3 implements plus valves for two or three remote hydraulic cylinders was optional.

An isolated, self-contained, capsule cab was standard equipment and reduced the noise level to 87.5 dB(A) during the 10-hour test at Nebraska. A separate 25-gpm pump was used for the steering system which operated the two hydraulic cylinders between the two frame units. The double disc brakes were hydraulically operated by one foot pedal.

Illustrating the advantages of a four-wheel-drive model, the Oliver 2655 was tested without ballast at Nebraska in June 1971. During the maximum power runs of Test 1070 it recorded 129.48 drawbar horsepower and 143.27 PTO horsepower.

Options for the Oliver 2655 included a 3-point hitch and a 1,000-rpm independent PTO which increased its versatility

The four-wheel drive enabled the unballasted 2655 to pull large semi-mounted plows.

Oliver 1265 & 1365
1971-1975

Two diesel-powered utility tractors, the 1265 and the 1365, were new for 1972. The 1265 was based on first the Fiat 450 and then the Fiat 480. The 1365 was first the Fiat 600 and then the Fiat 640. The two new models with increased power replaced the 1255 and 1355, but retained the Oliver family appearance with a white grill with a checkerboard pattern. The 1265 and the 1365 were available as two-wheel-drive utility tractors or with a front-wheel drive. Also there was a row-crop version of the 1365 with 25 inches of clearance under the adjustable front axle.

The new power levels of 41 and 55 PTO horsepower were obtained by increasing the bore of the Fiat engines to 3.94 inches from 3.74 inches. The stroke remained at 4.33 inches, so the displacements increased

The Fiat-built Oliver 1265 and 1365 had engines with increased displacements which raised the power levels to 41 and 55 PTO horsepower.

to 158 cubic inches for the 3-cylinder engine in the 1265 and to 211 cubic inches for the 4-cylinder engine in the 1365.

The 1265 retained the 6-speed transmission with speeds from 1.5 to 15.4 mph with 13.6-28 rear tires. The dual stage transmission in the 1365 provided eight speeds from 1.5 to 15.5 mph with 16.9-30 rear tires. Optional creeper gears provided a low speed of about 0.5 mph.

Both models continued to be equipped with a PTO drive that provided the 540-rpm speed or a ground speed which was timed with the rear wheels. The 540-rpm PTO was the live type on the 1265 and independent on the 1365. The 3-point hitch could now be set to provide draft control, position control, or float for semi-mounted implements.

Optional equipment included a roll bar, canopy for the roll bar, power adjustable rear wheels, a deluxe seat with backrest, belt pulley, and power steering for the 1265 two-wheel drive version.

The 1265 and 1365 were not tested at Nebraska.

The 1465 was a new size of utility tractor with 70 PTO horsepower.

A third utility model, the 1465, was added to the Oliver tractor line for 1973. It was built by Fiat and was equivalent to their 750 model, with 70 PTO horsepower in a compact package. Appearance and styling were similar to the 1265 and 1365 models.

The direct injection 4-cylinder Fiat diesel engine for the 1465 had both a larger bore and stroke than the

Oliver 1465
1973-1975

engines used in the 1265 and 1365, but the same 17 to 1 compression ratio. The bore was 4.33 inches and the stroke was 4.71 inches for a displacement of 278 cubic inches. The crankshaft was dynamically balanced and supported by five main bearings. A preheater and a 12-volt starting system worked together for quick starts on cold mornings.

The dual range transmission with two shift levers provided seven forward speeds and two in reverse. With 18.4-30 rear tires, five of the forward speeds were in a practical working range of 1.5 to 6.3 mph plus a "rotary hoe speed" of 9.1 mph and a transport speed of 15.0 mph. The 540 rpm PTO was the independent type. The 3-point hitch was adjustable for Category 1 or 2 implements and provided draft, position, or float control.

Operator comfort and convenience started with a deep-cushion seat with semi-circle arm rests and back support. Power steering and a foot accelerator assisted with front loader work. Turning one button released the grill for easy access to the air cleaner and batteries located between the grill and radiator. A roll bar and a canopy for the roll bar were optional.

The Oliver 1465 was not tested at the Nebraska Laboratory.

Oliver 2255
1972-1976

The Oliver 2255 was the last tractor manufactured at the Charles City, Iowa, factory with the Oliver name plate. Introduced in August 1972 as "new for 1973," the 2255 was the only Oliver tractor with a V-8 engine and was the most powerful Oliver two-wheel-drive tractor built with 145 PTO horsepower. Its styling matched that of its five smaller brothers in Oliver's line of row-crop tractors. It was available in two versions, the row-crop with an adjustable front axle with more than 24 inches of clearance and the all-wheel-drive version with a mechanically driven front-wheel drive.

At first the 2255 was powered with a Caterpillar V-8 diesel engine with 573 cubic inches of displacement, resulting from a 4.50- x 4.50-inch bore and stroke. With a rated engine speed of 2,600 rpm, the engine featured strong lugging power down to 1,600 rpm with a 17-percent torque rise. Caterpillar then replaced the 573-cubic-inch engine with a 636-cubic-inch V-8 engine with a 4.50- x 5.00-inch bore and stroke and it was used to power the later 2255 models. The 2255 followed the Oliver tradition by mounting the engine in a cast frame which provided strength and extra weight for the front of the tractor.

The power train used a constant mesh helical gear transmission with six forward speeds and two in reverse as standard equipment. Optional was the additional Over/Under Hydraul-Shift transmission which provided three speeds—under drive, direct drive, and over drive—with on-the-go shifting for each of the regular gears for a total of 18 forward speeds and six in reverse. Nine of the forward speeds were in the working range of 2 to 6 mph. Planetaries were used at the outboard end of the rear axles to reduce the torque load on the axles.

The independent 1,000-rpm PTO was controlled with a hydraulic clutch. A dual speed PTO was optional. The hydraulic functions were built around a 2,200 psi closed center system. The 3-point hitch was operated with two external cylinders which could lift up to 6,000 pound Category 2 or 3 implements. Also the 2250 could be equipped with remote circuits for up to four remote hydraulic cylinders.

The operator's station was similar to the other large Oliver models with an isolated platform, a deep cushioned seat with a steel torsion bar suspension, a power steering system that tilted to four positions and telescoped to six positions, and hydraulic powered triple disc brakes.

A new optional factory-installed cab was equipped with two roll bars to provide roll over protection. It was mounted on rubber isolation blocks to absorb shocks and vibration. To reduce the sound level, the cab was built with neoprene seals for the doors, a 1-inch thick headliner, and a foam-padded rubber floor mat. The noise level at the operator's ear was 89.0 dB(A) during the 10-hour test at Nebraska. The incoming air was filtered and could be heated or air conditioned. This cab could also be installed on the 1755, 1855, and 1955 models.

The Oliver 2255 with the 573-cubic-inch V-8 engine was tested at the Nebraska Tractor Test Lab in September 1973. It was equipped with dual 18.4-38 rear tires for the test. The results of Test 1140 were 126.13 maximum drawbar horsepower and 146.72 maximum PTO horsepower.

The last Oliver model introduced was the 2255, a large two-wheel-drive tractor which usually was equipped with dual rear tires and a cab.

The Oliver 2255 was powered with Caterpillar V-8 engines, the first one with 573 cubic inches of displacement and then one with 636 cubic inches.

White — A New Name, Colors, and Styling

White Field Boss 4-150 & White Field Boss 4-180

1974-1978 & 1975-1978

The experimental version of the 4-150 was known as the Low Profile 4WD tractor and was painted Oliver green and white. Here the center pivot oscillation is being checked.

In July 1973 a four-wheel-drive tractor with a unique configuration rolled out of the experimental shop at the Charles City, Iowa, factory. This prototype tractor was built much lower than other four-wheel-drive tractors, with the engine positioned ahead of the front axle and with a cab height that was similar to two-wheel-drive tractors. The styling was also completely different with a silver and charcoal paint scheme. The White name in large block letters was positioned over the silver stripes on the sides of the hood. Soon this tractor, which replaced the Oliver 2655, was introduced to the dealers as the new Field Boss 4-150 with 150 PTO horsepower and production started in 1974.

The 4-150 was built in response to farmer requests, the first demand was for maximum traction. As a result the 4-150 was a four-wheel-drive tractor with the weight distributed evenly between the two axles when it was under load. The next request was for adjustable wheel tread for varying crop and row widths, so the wheel tread of the 4-150 was adjustable from 58 to 108 inches. The third request was for a short turning radius and the articulated frame of the 4-150 with the 30 degrees of oscillation at the center pivot permitted the tractor to turn in small areas.

Farmers requested a 3-point hitch for a variety of implements, so the 4-150 could be equipped with a heavy-duty 3-point hitch with a lift capacity of 6,000 pounds for Category 2 or 3 implements. Large fuel capacity was the next request and the 4-150 was equipped with a 94-gallon fuel tank. Visibility was high on the farmers' list, so the 4-150 was built with the muffler and air cleaner intake under the hood, glass panels in the lower part of the cab, and a large rear window. Along with visibility was the request for comfort which the 4-150 answered with its new modular, ROPS-equipped cab which was isolated from the tractor's vibration and noise. A wide selection of speeds was another request, so the Over/Under Hydraul-Shift with 18 forward speeds was available for the 4-150.

The power plant for this new tractor was a 636-cubic-inch Caterpillar V-8 diesel engine. The power from the engine was transmitted to the Hydraul-Shift and then to a drive shaft which was in line with both axles. A 1,000-rpm independent PTO and two valves and outlets for remote cylinders were standard equipment.

A very similar four-wheel-drive model, the 4-180, was introduced the following year and it was rated at 180 PTO horsepower. The 4-180 also used the 636-cubic-inch Caterpillar V-8 diesel engine, but was set for a higher output. The extra power did result in a different helical gear transmission with 12 forward speeds and the use of outboard planetaries to reduce the torque loads in the axles. Thus the wheel tread settings for the 4-180 were limited to five settings. The 18.4-38 dual tires were standard, but the 4-180 could be equipped with 18.4-38 or 23.1-34 singles. The new modular cab exhibited its quality design during the 10-hour test at Nebraska with the noise level at the operator's ear being a very respectable 83.5 dB(A).

Both the 4-150 and the 4-180 were equipped with dual wheels, but no extra ballast, for their tests at Nebraska in May 1974 and August 1975, respectively. The results of these tests were:

The production 4-150 had a different hood, grill, color, and name, but the cab and other components appear to have been used without any major changes.

Model	Test No.	Type of Test	Drawbar Hp	PTO Hp
White 4-150 Diesel	1159	Maximum	133.34	151.87
White 4-180 Diesel	1184	Maximum	156.54	181.07

The first White two-wheel-drive tractor was the 2-105, with the first one driven off the assembly line in 1974.

White Field Boss 2-105 & White Field Boss 2-150

1974-1982 & 1975-1976

In addition to the 4-180, two new row-crop models with adjustable front axles were announced in 1974 as being "new for 1975." The 2-105 was rated at 105 PTO horsepower and the 2-150 at 145 PTO horsepower. These two White Field Boss models were the first two-wheel-drive tractors with the new silver and charcoal colors and the new White styling. Since they replaced the Oliver 1855, 1955, and 2255 models, the White tractor line for 1975 consisted of three Oliver utility models, three Oliver mid-size models, two larger White two-wheel-drive models, and two White four-wheel-drive models.

Factory-installed cabs for tractors were still optional, but they were becoming more popular and were being designed more as an integral part of the tractor. As a result, the 2-105 and 2-150 featured a new cab with a three-sided front for improved visibility and a built-in 4-post protective frame for safety. To reduce noise and vibration, the cab was isolated with rubber mounts. During the 10-hour test at Nebraska, the noise level at the operator's ear was 88.5 dB(A) for the 2-105 and 90.0 dB(A) for the 2-150.

Other features for the operator's comfort included the adjustable seat on the inclined mounting rail, power steering with the Tilt-O-Scope steer-ing wheel, and hydraulically-powered disc brakes. A roll-over protective frame, canopy, and fender fuel tanks were available for open platform tractors.

The 2-105 was powered with a turbocharged version of the Perkins 6-cylinder diesel engine with the 354-cubic-inch displacement which had been used previously. The rated engine speed was 2,200 rpm. The engine for the 2-150, now described as a White 6-cylinder, 585-cubic-inch diesel engine, was the former Minneapolis-Moline engine used in the Oliver 2155 and 2655 models. It still had a 4.75- x 5.50-inch bore and stroke and a rated engine speed of 2,200 rpm.

Both models continued to be equipped with a helical gear transmission with six forward speeds and two in reverse. Optional was the Over/Under Hydraul-Shift package which provided three on-the-go shifting speeds in each of the regular gears. With this partial powershift transmission, the travel speeds ranged from about 1.5 to 18.0 mph with nine in the 2 to 6 mph working range.

The PTO for both models continued to be the independent type with a hydraulic clutch. The dual 540/1,000 rpm PTO was standard for the 2-105 and optional for the 2-150. The standard PTO for the higher horsepower 2-150 was the 1,000 rpm. Both models featured closed center hydraulics with the 3-point hitch being a Category 2 for the 2-105 and a Category 3 with 6,000 pounds of lifting capacity for the 2-150.

A new feature for the White two-wheel-drive tractors was the cab with the three-sided front. A pressurizer and heater were standard; air conditioning was optional.

The White 2-105 and 2-150 models were tested at the Nebraska Tractor Test Lab in June 1975. The results of the tests of the 2-105 equipped with 20.8-38 rear tires and the 2-150 with its dual 18.4-38 rear tires were:

Model	Test No.	Type of Test	Drawbar Hp	PTO Hp
White Field Boss 2-105 Diesel	1181	Maximum	90.81	105.61
White Field Boss 2-150 Diesel	1182	Maximum	127.49	147.49

This White 2-70 with ROPS and canopy shows the new White styling was revised to include two headlights in the top of the grill.

In 1975 two more models, the 2-70 and the 2-85, were added to the Field Boss line of tractors replacing the Oliver 1555, 1655, and 1755. Production started in late 1975 for the 2-85 and early in 1976 for the 2-70. Front axles included an adjustable front axle, a fixed tread front axle, or a front-wheel drive.

The power plant for the 2-70 was the 6-cylinder, 283-cubic-inch diesel engine or the 6-cylinder, 265-cubic-inch gasoline engine, the same sizes as the engines for the 1650 and 1655. The gasoline engine was dropped by 1980. The 2-85 was powered with the 6-cylinder, 354-cubic-inch Perkins diesel engine, the same size as the one for the Oliver 1850, and was the naturally aspirated version of the turbocharged one in the 2-105.

White Field Boss 2-70 & White Field Boss 2-85

1976-1982 & 1975-1982

Both models used a constant mesh, helical gear transmission with the usual six forward speeds and the Over/Under Hydraul-Shift package was optional. The standard PTO for the 2-70 was 540 rpm and the dual speed PTO was optional. The 2-85 used the dual speed PTO as standard.

The hydraulics for the 2-70 were the open center type and its 3-point hitch was the Category 2 size. The 2-85 was a 2-105 with a smaller engine, so it had the closed center hydraulic system, hydraulic powered brakes, and a Category 2 size of 3-point hitch. The new cab with the three-sided front was optional for the 2-85.

The White Field Boss 2-70 and 2-85 were tested at Nebraska in May 1976 and the following results were similar to the 1970 tests of the Oliver 1655 and 1755 tractors.

Model	Test No.	Type of Test	Drawbar Hp	PTO Hp
White Field Boss 2-70 Diesel	1212	Maximum	59.47	70.71
White Field Boss 2-85 Diesel	1213	Maximum	71.93	85.54

White Field Boss 2-50 & White Field Boss 2-60

1976-1980 & 1976-1979

Early in 1976 the line of Oliver tractors became history after 46 years of existence as two new White tractors replaced the Oliver 1265, 1365, and 1465 models. Just like the models they replaced, the new White Field Boss 2-50 and 2-60 were utility models built by Fiat in Italy, corresponding to the Fiat 500 and 640, respectively. The styling was revised to closely match that of the tractors built in Charles City, including two headlights in the grill.

The power levels were increased from 41 to 46 and from 55 to 59 PTO horsepower, but the size of the Fiat engines remained the same. The 2-50 was equipped with the 3-cylinder, 158-cubic-inch diesel engine and the 2-60 was powered with the 4-cylinder, 211-cubic-inch diesel engine. The rated engine speed of the 2-50 was increased to 2,500 rpm.

The two models became more similar as both now had the 8-speed transmission which previously was provided only in the 1365. Also the independent 540 rpm PTO was now standard on both models, as was power steering. Optional equipment included a mechanical front-wheel drive, power adjustable rear wheels, and a creeper gear set with an additional four slower speeds.

For the first time, the utility tractors sold by White were tested at Nebraska. The results of the March 1977 tests revealed more power than originally estimated, especially for the 2-60.

Model	Test No.	Type of Test	Drawbar Hp	PTO Hp
White Field Boss 2-50 Diesel	1231	Maximum	41.88	47.02
White Field Boss 2-60 Diesel	1232	Maximum	54.78	63.22

The White 2-50 and 2-60 were equipped with a new 4-post roll-over protective structure and canopy.

White Field Boss 2-135 & White Field Boss 2-155

1976-1982

After five years of market research and engineering effort to insure their acceptance by the nation's large acreage farmers, White announced the Field Boss 2-135 and the 2-155 tractors with an estimated 135 and 155 PTO horsepower, respectively. New for 1977, both models featured the new Field Boss styling, but with head lights in the top of the grill and no single vertical bar on the grill.

The biggest changes were in the cab which was now standard equipment. It was mounted on six new variable rate rubber mounts for a smoother ride. To reduce the noise level, perforated acoustical foam was used throughout the interior of the cab, the speed of the engine fan was reduced, and the air conditioner fan was relocated. As a result the noise level inside the cab was reduced at the Nebraska tests from 90.0 dB(A) for the 2-150 to 79.5 dB(A) for the 2-155. This reduction of 10 points on the dB(A) scale means the noise level inside the cab for the 2-155 was only one-half the level of the 2-150.

Other major changes inside the cab were a deluxe arm rest seat with the appearance of an office chair and a new console located to the right of the seat with the main gear shift lever, park lock, PTO, and hydraulic controls. A new electronic monitor on the dash provided a digital readout of ground

The White 2-135 was a new size and the 2-155 replaced the 2-150. The cab was improved to lower the sound level to one-half of that in the 2-150.

speed, engine speed, and PTO speed. The cab still provided a built-in roll-over protective structure for safety, a three-sided front for visibility, and Tilt-O-Scope power steering for maximum comfort.

Both models were powered with the same engine, a turbocharged 6-cylinder White Hercules diesel engine with 478 cubic inches of displacement. The bore and stroke were 4.56 x 4.87 inches and the rated engine speed was 2,200 rpm. Different fuel injection pumps were used to obtain the two power levels.

The proven 18-speed Over/Under Hydraul-Shift transmission was standard on these models to ensure they would provide the desired productivity. There were three powershift speeds in each of the six forward gears with the speeds ranging from 2.2 to 17.8 mph with 18.4-38 rear tires. The final drive had been redesigned to include inboard planetaries to reduce the strain on the drive gears and the rear axles were now 3.88 inches in diameter. A differential lock could be engaged on-the-go.

An independent 1,000 rpm PTO was standard for both models, but the dual speed PTO was optional for the 2-135. The closed center hydraulic system was advertised as the industry's most advanced hydraulic system. The 3-point hitch included a quick coupler which was a Category 3 size with a 6,400-pound lift capacity, measured 24 inches behind the hitch points.

Optional equipment included rear tires ranging from 18.4-38 to 24.5-32, dual wheels, power adjustable wheels, front satchel weights, and rear wheel weights. A mechanically powered front-wheel drive became available in 1978.

The performance of the 2-135 and 2-155 were measured at the Nebraska Laboratory in May 1978 with the following results:

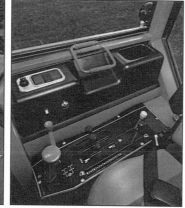

Operator convenience was improved with a new electronic monitor located on the right end of the dash and a control console positioned next to the seat.

Model	Test No.	Type of Test	Drawbar Hp	PTO Hp
White Field Boss 2-135 Diesel	1275	Maximum	117.67	137.64
White Field Boss 2-155 Diesel	1276	Maximum	139.68	157.73

White Field Boss 2-180
1977-1982

Undoubtedly one of the requests received in the extensive field survey of large acreage farmers was the need for a larger row-crop tractor. White introduced the 2-180 with an estimated 180 PTO horsepower as "new for 1978" and production started in late 1977. The 2-180 followed the Oliver tradition of providing built-in weight to match the horsepower, so it had a base shipping weight of 16,000 pounds.

Also "new for 1978" was a front-wheel drive for the 2-180, the 2-155, and the 2-135. This factory-installed option was the mechanical drive type with planetary gears in the wheel hubs.

The 2-180 was a big brother to the 2-155 and 2-135, so the styling and many of the features were shared by all three models. The 2-180 featured the same cab, seat, and con-

The new White 2-180 with 181 PTO horsepower established a new power level for an Oliver or White two-wheel-drive tractor.

trols as the other two models. The 3 x 6 Over/Under transmission was just a new name for the traditional Over/Under Hydraul-Shift transmission with three powershift speeds in each of six gears. The drive train also used the inboard planetary final drives and the 3.88 inch diameter rear axles.

The diesel power plant for the 2-180 was the Caterpillar 3208 V-8 engine with a displacement of 636 cubic inches and a rated speed of 2,800 rpm. The engine delivered 210 engine horsepower and provided a 23-percent torque rise.

The White Field Boss 2-180 was tested with dual tires and without additional ballast at Nebraska in September 1978. Its performance in Test 1287 was 163.64 maximum drawbar horsepower and 181.89 maximum PTO horsepower.

White Field Boss 4-210
1978-1982

The White Field Boss 4-210 was introduced at the January 1978 dealer meeting in Orlando as the replacement for the 4-180. However, the 4-210 did not represent an increase of 30 horsepower because there was no change in the Caterpillar V-8 engine and the model number for this four-wheel drive tractor now represented its engine horsepower.

The new model number was the result of changes to the transmission and many other components. The 12-speed transmission used in the 4-180 was replaced with a 3 x 6 Over/Under transmission, a 6-speed transmission with the traditional over/under powershift package. The planetary final drives were moved to an inboard position which provided an adjustable wheel tread. The center frame hinge was turned upside down with the ball joint now at the top. This moved it away from the dirt for longer life and provided more operator comfort as it was now closer to the operator's station. Also it was made 30-percent stronger.

The design of the cab now included the latest improvements provided in the row-crop models which reduced the sound level inside the the cab to 81.0 dB(A) at Nebraska. The seat was the office chair type and a restyled console was provided to the right of the operator. The dash now provided a 14-channel electronic monitoring display and an 8-channel digital display of speeds and temperatures. Night visibility was improved by adding two head lights at the top of the grill.

The 4-210 wasn't tested at Nebraska until June 1979. Then in Test 1318 it recorded 162.25 maximum drawbar horsepower, while equipped with dual 18.4-38 tires and no extra ballast, and 182.44 PTO horsepower.

With the 4-210, White started using engine horsepower to establish the model number of their four-wheel-drive tractors.

White Iseki Field Boss 2-30 & 2-35
1979-1984

The 2-30 and 2-35 models were the first utility tractors built for Oliver or White by Iseki of Japan.

White added Iseki of Japan as a second supplier of utility tractors in 1979. The first two models were the 2-30 and 2-35 which were introduced to the dealers in early 1979 at their meeting in San Antonio, Texas. These compact tractors were estimated to produce 27 and 31 PTO horsepower, respectively. The silver and charcoal colors were used, but both the White and Iseki names appeared over the silver stripes on the hood sides.

Both models were powered with 3-cylinder Isuzu diesel engines which were equipped with glow plugs for easy starting. Both engines used a 3.39-inch bore. The 3.39-inch stroke for the 2-30 resulted in a 91-cubic-inch displacement and the 4.02-inch stroke on the 2-35 provided 108 cubic inches. The transmission with two gear shift levers provided eight forward speeds by using a High/Low range selector and a 4-speed gearbox. The speeds ranged from about 0.8 to 12 mph.

The live 540-rpm PTO was controlled with the 2-stage clutch pedal. The 3-point hitch offered only position control. The foot accelerator and differential lock were standard and power steering was optional. A mechanical front-wheel drive with power steering was available for the 2-30. A 2-post ROPS and seat belt were available for both models.

The 2-30 and 2-35 were tested at the Nebraska Tractor Testing Lab in October and November 1980 and produced the following power levels:

Model	Test No.	Type of Test	Drawbar Hp	PTO Hp
White Iseki 2-30 Diesel	1373	Maximum	25.81	28.33
White Iseki 2-35 Diesel	1374	Maximum	30.37	32.84

The White advertised the 4-175 as a row-crop tractor which could pull both plows and cultivators.

The 4-150 was updated and became the 4-175, with production starting August 17, 1979. And again the new model number reflected the 175 engine horsepower, because the power level of the 636-cubic-inch Caterpillar V-8 diesel engine did not change.

The 4-175 was updated with the many of the same features as the 4-210. The articulation joint was turned upside down to place the ball joint at the top which improved the life of the ball joint and provided a more comfortable ride for the operator. The wheel tread could be adjusted from 60 to 108 inches by moving the wheels on the 3.19-inch diameter axles. The 4-175 still had 18 forward speeds, ranging from 1.6 to 19 mph, with the 3 x 6 Over/Under transmission.

White Field Boss 4-175
1979-1982

The cab was similar to the ones used on the other large White tractors, with sound-absorbing insulation around the interior, an office chair type seat, and the restyled console next to the operator. The dash now included the 8-channel digital display of speeds and temperatures and the 14-channel electronic monitoring display which warned of any malfunction.

Unlike many of the four-wheel-drive tractors on the market at this time, the 4-175 provided an independent PTO, a 3-point hitch, and two sets of remote hydraulic outlets as standard equipment. Also the standard lighting package included four head lights and four rear flood lights plus warning lights and tail lights.

The 4-175 was tested at Nebraska in November 1980 with dual 18.4-38 tires, but without extra ballast. The maximum power results were almost identical with those of the 4-150 in May 1974, being 133.72 drawbar horsepower and 151.69 PTO horsepower.

White Iseki Field Boss 2-45 & 2-62

1979-1981

White changed its source of utility tractors in 1980 by adding two more models from Iseki and dropping the Fiat-sourced 2-50 and 2-60. The new models were the 2-45 with an estimated 43 PTO horsepower and the 2-62 with an estimated 60 PTO horsepower. The styling was very similar to the larger models in the White line. However, these two tractors had engine side panels.

The 2-45 was powered with a 4-cylinder Isuzu diesel engine with 169 cubic inches, resulting from a 3.86- x 3.62-inch bore and stroke. The engine for the 2-62 was also a 4-cylinder Isuzu diesel, but with a 4.02- x 4.33-inch bore and stroke for a displacement of 219 cubic inches. Both engines were equipped with glow plugs for cold weather starting.

Iseki became White's only utility tractor supplier when the 2-45 and 2-62 were added to the line.

The unique power train used a 5-speed gearbox coupled to two 2-speed range transmissions to provide 20 forward speeds. The shift levers with their T-handles for the range transmissions were located to the left of the operator's seat and could be shifted together with one hand or individually. The resulting forward speeds ranged from 0.2 to about 15 mph.

The PTO could be set to be an independent type with a hydraulic clutch or a ground-driven type. The 3-point hitch was the Category 2 size. Optional equipment included a front-wheel drive, power adjustable rear wheels, a 2-post ROPS with a seat belt, and a canopy.

The results of the Nebraska tests in June 1981 for these two utility tractors were:

Model	Test No.	Type of Test	Drawbar Hp	PTO Hp
White Iseki 2-45 Diesel	1395	Maximum	37.22	43.73
White Iseki 2-62 Diesel	1396	Maximum	51.63	61.46

In May 1976 White Consolidated Industries and the White Motor Corporation were planning to merge, but the plans collapsed the day before the stockholders were to vote on the merger. This situation left the future of White Motor in doubt, as it had lost $69 million in 1975 and its share of the truck market was declining. Although there was speculation White Motor would sell its White Farm Equipment division to ease its financial crisis, the parent company resolved its situation by selling the Euclid line of off-highway haulers and the Superior and White engine divisions.

A Corporate Crisis

1976-1981

In 1977 Consolidated Freightways Inc. took over the distribution of its Freightliner trucks and thus White Motor lost 40 percent of its truck sales. By September 1980 the White Motor Corporation simply ran out of money and was forced to file for reorganization under Chapter 11 of the federal bankruptcy code. Then in November White Motor announced it was selling its White Farm Equipment division to the TIC Investment Corporation of Dallas, Texas. Operations resumed in January 1981 at the South Bend, Indiana, implement factory and in March 1981 at the Charles City, Iowa, tractor plant.

For 1981 the tractor line continued with 12 models. There were four utility models built by Iseki, six models of two-wheel-drive row-crop tractors and two four-wheel-drive models which completed the line. The identification on the tractors changed to a wide red stripe on the sides of the hood and the WFE initials replaced the White name.

The line of utility tractors expanded by one model when the 2-55, 2-65, and 2-75 replaced the 2-45 and 2-62.

The new White Farm Equipment Company (WFE) introduced four new tractor models in the spring of 1982. Three were utility models built in Japan by Iseki — the 2-55, the 2-6.5, and the 2-75.

The three power plants were Isuzu diesels which were built around a common bore diameter of 4.02 inches. The 4-cylinder engine for the 2-55 had a 3.94-inch stroke and the 2-65 had a 4.65-inch stroke for its 4-cylinder engine. The 2-75 was powered with a 6-cylinder version of the replaced 2-62's engine with a 4.33-inch stroke. Each model provided 16 forward speeds and four in reverse by combining a 4-speed synchromesh transmission with a 2-speed auxiliary and a 2-speed creeper.

The 3-point hitches were the Category 2 size and one remote hydraulic valve was standard. The 2-55 and 2-65 had an independent 540 rpm PTO and the 2-75 was equipped with a dual speed independent PTO. Ground speed PTO was also provided. The operator's platform was flat and power steering was standard. A 2-post ROPS with seat belt, a canopy, power adjustable rear wheels, and a mechanically driven front-wheel drive were optional.

The 2-55 and 2-65 were tested at Nebraska in April 1983 and the 2-75 was tested in September 1983. The results of these three tests were:

WFE Field Boss 2-55, 2-65, & 2-75
1982-1987

Model	Test No.	Type of Test	Drawbar Hp	PTO Hp
WFE Field Boss 2-55 Diesel	1466	Maximum	48.49	53.32
WFE Field Boss 2-65 Diesel	1467	Maximum	56.67	62.50
WFE Field Boss 2-75 Diesel	1486	Maximum	65.05	75.39

WFE Field Boss 2-88 & 2-110
1982-1987

The WFE 2-110 was the fourth model introduced in the spring of 1982. Then in the August 1982 WFE introduced the 2-88 as "new for 1983." The 2-110 replaced the 2-105 and the 2-88 replaced the 2-85 and 2-70. Both models were available with an adjustable front axle or the Power Front Axle, WFE's name for their front-wheel drive.

Except for the red hood stripe and the WFE identification, the styling did not change. The 2-110 and the 2-88 had the new modular cab in which the cab, steering column, and controls became one integrated unit, separate from the rest of the tractor to keep noise and vibration to a minimum. There was a new right side console with the hydraulic, shift, and throttle controls.

Both models were powered with improved versions of the 354-cubic-

The WFE 2-110 was introduced in the spring of 1982 and by 1984 it was WFE's best-selling model.

inch, 6-cylinder Perkins diesel engine which had been used in the 2-105 and 2-85. As before, the engine for the 2-110 was turbocharged and the engine for the 2-88 was naturally aspirated. The transmission for both models was the Over/Under transmission with three powershift speeds in each of the six forward gears.

In its tests at Nebraska in April 1983, the 2-110 demonstrated its improved engine by recording an outstanding PTO fuel efficiency of 16.77 hp-hr/gal. The 2-88 also established a new record for Oliver and White tractors with a sound level of only 75.5 dB(A) during the 10-hour test. The other performance results were:

Model	Test No.	Type of Test	Drawbar Hp	PTO Hp
WFE Field Boss 2-88 Diesel	1487	Maximum	74.67	86.78
WFE Field Boss 2-110 Diesel	1468	Maximum	94.90	110.52

WFE Field Boss 4-225 & 4-270
1983-1987 & 1983-1988

The other two tractors introduced in August 1982 at the dealers' meeting in Charles City, Iowa, were new four-wheel-drive models, the 4-225 and 4-270. As indicated by the model numbers, the power rating of the engines were an estimated 225 and 270 horsepower. The 4-225 replaced the 4-175 and 4-210, but its styling and configuration were very similar to the replaced models. Its wheel tread was adjustable and this four-wheel-drive tractor could be used for row-crop work. The 4-270 featured a new larger articulated frame and had a shipping weight of 29,060 pounds. Its styling was similar to the 4-225, but its wider hood and grill and its larger tires gave it a more massive appearance.

The major change for the 4-225 was the engine which was a turbocharged version of the Caterpillar 636-cubic-inch V-8 diesel engine. The drive train continued to use the 3 x 6 Over/Under transmission. The final drive utilized inboard planetaries and the front and rear differential lock could be engaged on-the-go.

The 4-270 was powered with a Caterpillar in-line, 6-cylinder diesel engine with a

The WFE 4-225 added a turbocharger to its Caterpillar V-8 engine to increase its engine power output to 225 horsepower.

638-cubic-inch displacement. This was the first engine used in an Oliver or White tractor which was turbocharged and aftercooled. With the more powerful engine there was a need for a stronger transmission, so the 4-270 featured a new 4 x 4 powershift transmission which was 10 years in development. This transmission had four powershift speeds in each of four forward gears and the one in reverse, thus providing 16 forward speeds and four in reverse.

The modular cab was isolated from the remainder of the tractor and was lined with sound-deadening insulation to reduce the

A new 4 x 4 powershift transmission was required for the additional power developed by the WFE 4-270.

noise level. The result was new records at Nebraska for White four-wheel-drive tractors of 78.0 dB(A) for the 4-225 and 78.5 dB(A) for the 4-270.

Unlike many competitive four-wheel-drive tractors, an independent 1,000 rpm PTO was standard equipment for both models. The 4-225 was equipped with a Category 3, draft-controlled 3-point hitch and two remote hydraulic valves. The 4-270 provided a swinging drawbar as standard equipment, but a larger Category 4 size of 3-point hitch was available as an option. Three sets of remote hydraulic outlets were standard and a fourth was optional.

Soon after the 4-225 and 4-270 were introduced in August 1982, the Charles City factory stopped assembling tractors due to financial problems. After a new financing agreement with Borg-Warner was announced in May 1983, the factory reopened in August 1983. The first 4-225 rolled off the assembly line in October 1983 and the first 4-270 was produced in November 1983. However, it was April 1985 before the two models were tested at Nebraska. The 4-270 established a new record for fuel efficiency for White four-wheel-drive tractors of 16.52 hp-hr/gal during the PTO tests. The results of the power tests were:

Model	Test No.	Type of Test	Drawbar Hp	PTO Hp
WFE Field Boss 4-225 Diesel	1558	Maximum	170.57	195.65
WFE Field Boss 4-270 Diesel	1559	Maximum	211.70	239.25

WFE 2-135, 2-155, & 2-180 Series 3
1982-1987

The two-wheel-drive tractors with the new modular cabs were identified by the Series 3 under the model number.

The Series 3 versions of the 2-135, 2-155, and 2-180 were introduced as "new for 1983." Although they were never identified or labeled, the Series 1 versions were the original tractors with the White name on the hood sides and the Series 2 versions were those with the red hood stripe and the WFE identification.

The major improvement for the Series 3 tractors was the modular cab which improved operator comfort. With this type of cab, the steering column and controls became part of the cab and were isolated from the rest of the tractor. The new cab included an improved air conditioner, a powerful heater, and a pressurization system to keep out the dust.

The fully adjustable seat was positioned over the rear axle for a better ride. A new console was located to the right of the seat and the dash was used only for instruments.

The Series 3 models were advertised with their "official PTO horsepower" (the Nebraska tests for Series 1), so their ratings increased slightly to 137, 157, and 181 PTO horsepower. The engines remained the White Hercules turbocharged 6-

By the mid-1980s a typical large two-wheel-drive tractor included dual rear wheels and a factory-installed cab.

cylinder diesel engine for the 2-135 and the 2-155. The 2-180 continued to use the 636-cubic-inch V-8 Caterpillar engine and the 3 x 6 Over/Under transmission. The three Series 3 models could be equipped with an adjustable front axle or the Power Front Axle.

One new model with a 4-cylinder engine, the 2-32, replaced two models with 3-cylinder engines, the 2-30 and the 2-35. The 2-32 was rated at 28 PTO horsepower and was built in Japan by Iseki. The styling was somewhat different with a horizontal slot type of grill. However, the engine side panels were still used. This compact tractor could be equipped with an adjustable front axle or a front-wheel drive.

WFE Field Boss 2-32
1985-1986

The Isuzu diesel engine had a rated speed of 2,600 rpm and a displacement of 90.7 cubic inches, resulting from a 3.0- x 3.2-inch bore and stroke. A glow plug was provided to assist with cold weather starting. The standard drive train was a 3-speed synchromesh transmission with a 3-speed auxiliary and a 2-speed creeper range. This combination provided 18 forward speeds.

The independent 540 rpm PTO had a unique control system. If a gradual engagement was desired, the electric control was set to "on" and the hydraulic control was used to slowly engage the PTO. If a gradual engagement

With the introduction of the WFE 2-32, the smallest utility tractor in the line was powered by a 4-cylinder engine.

was not required, the hydraulic control was fully engaged and the electric control on the dash was used to engage or disengage the PTO. The Category 1 size of 3-point hitch had a lift capacity of 2,700 pounds.

The 2-32 featured power steering, a tilt steering wheel, hand and foot throttles, a differential lock, and a 2-post ROPS with seat belt as standard equipment. Optional equipment included a canopy for the ROPS and a fender-mounted radio.

The WFE Field Boss 2-32 tractor was not tested at Nebraska.

Since small tractors now accounted for over 50 percent of the U.S. tractor sales, White added compact models such as the FB 16.

The FB 31 with 25 PTO horsepower represented the middle size in the new line of five models of compact tractors.

New White Field Boss Compacts
1986-1989

In March 1985 Borg-Warner demanded payment of its loans to WFE and soon WFE was forced into bankruptcy. Then in September 1985 Allied Products Corporation purchased White Farm Equipment. The first new tractors Allied introduced in June 1986 were five models of compact tractors which replaced the 2-32 model. Iseki continued to be the source for these compact models.

The appearance of the five new models was similar to the 2-32, but they used a black stripe on the sides of the hood instead of the red stripe used since 1981. The four largest models were equipped with engine side panels. Each model could be equipped with an adjustable front axle or a front-wheel drive. A 2-post ROPS was standard equipment.

The two smallest models were powered with 3-cylinder diesel engines. The Field Boss 16 with 16 engine horsepower and 14 PTO horsepower had a displacement of 51.8 cubic inches. The Field Boss 21 stepped up to 21 engine horsepower and 19 PTO horsepower with its 71.4-cubic-inch engine. The transmission for the Field Boss 16 had six forward speeds and two in reverse. The Field Boss 21 provided 12 forward speeds and 4 in reverse. The PTO for these two models was driven by the transmission, so it was not live or independent. However, the hydraulic system was live and the 3-point hitch was the Category 1 size.

The Field Boss 31, with its 91.4-cubic-inch, 3-cylinder diesel engine, was rated at 30 engine horsepower and 25 PTO horsepower. The syn-chronized main transmission was combined with a range selection and a creeper gear to provide 12 forward speeds and 4 reverse speeds. The PTO was independent and was activated by either an electric switch or a hydraulic control. The 3-point hitch was the Category 1 size.

The two largest models were equipped with 4-cylinder diesel engines. The estimated power of the Field Boss 37 with its 110.8-cubic-inch displacement was 37 engine horsepower and 30 horsepower at the PTO. The 144.6-cubic-inch engine for the Field Boss 43 was rated at 45 engine horsepower and 39 PTO horsepower. All five models had the same rated speed of 2,600 rpm and a glow plug starting aid, but there was little commonality of bores and strokes. The transmission for the Field Boss 37 had 18 forward speeds and 6 in reverse, while the Field Boss 43 was equipped with 12 forward and 4 reverse speeds. The 540 rpm independent PTO was operated by an electric switch or a hydraulic control. The live hydraulic system operated the Category 1 size of 3-point hitch and one or two remote outlets.

Optional equipment included fender-mounted radios, a canopy for the ROPS, and a horizontal muffler.

These five compact tractors were not tested at Nebraska.

The two largest models, the FB 37 and FB 43, were powered with 4-cylinder diesel engines.

White Field Boss 185 and White 100, 120, 140, & 160
1986-1989 and 1987-1989

The White Field Boss 185 was also introduced in June 1986. It featured a 6-cylinder CDC-Cummins diesel engine and replaced the 2-180 with its Caterpillar V-8 engine. The estimated PTO power increased slightly to 185 horsepower with this 505-cubic-inch, turbocharged and aftercooled engine which featured a 31-percent torque rise.

During 1987 Allied Products combined their White and New Idea divisions into one company named White-New Idea Farm Equipment. For the 1988 model year, White-New Idea introduced four new models and a revised edition of the 185. All five models were now built around one brand of 6-cylinder diesel engine, CDC-Cummins. Identification was changed to a black stripe on the sides of the hood plus the White name and model number. The Field Boss name was discontinued.

The White 100 and 120 models were the replacements for the 2-88 and 2-110 models. The new power plant for the 100 and 120 was the C D C - C u m m i n s 359-cubic-inch engine, with the 100 being naturally aspirated and the 120 being turbocharged. The initial power ratings were 92 and 118 PTO horsepower, respectively, as compared to 86 and 110 for the replaced models.

The White 140 and White 160 replaced the 2-135 Series 3 and the 2-155 Series 3. The 140 with its 359-cubic-inch, turbocharged and aftercooled CDC-Cummins engine was initially rated at 137 PTO horsepower,

The new 185-PTO horsepower model was known as the White Field Boss 185 for one year and then became the White 185.

the same as the 2-135. The initial power rating of the 160 was 160 PTO horsepower, a slight increase over the 157 horsepower of the 2-155. The 160 stepped up to the next size of C D C - C u m m i n s engine with the turbocharged version of the 505-cubic-inch engine.

For 1988 the White Field Boss 185 became the White 185 when the Field Boss name was dropped.

Operator comfort

All models of the new White line of large two-wheel-drive tractors were powered with CDC-Cummins 6-cylinder diesel engines.

and convenience were also improved with this new tractor series. The interior of the cab was changed from bright red to a more subdued shade of gray. A new AeroForm air cushion seat with rocker action was optional. The new FieldFacts information system provided a digital readout of speeds and hours plus monitoring seven potential problem areas. When it was combined with the optional radar unit, it also provided data about ground speed, wheel slip, and acres covered. Sound levels inside the cab were reduced slightly.

A new PosiTrac Full Power Front Axle was optional for all five models. It provided a limited slip differential for improved tractive effort, a tighter turning radius, and better crop clearance. The five new tractors continued to use the 3 x 6 Over/Under partial powershift transmission.

The five models were tested at Nebraska in April and October 1988 with radial tires. The 160 set a new fuel efficiency record for White and Oliver tractors of 17.59 hp-hr/gal. The power results were:

Model	Test No.	Type of Test	Drawbar Hp	PTO Hp
White 100 Diesel	1614	Maximum	82.57	94.36
White 120 Diesel	1615	Maximum	104.69	119.13
White 140 Diesel	1616	Maximum	125.01	138.53
White 160 Diesel	1607	Maximum	142.74	162.47
White 185 Diesel	1608	Maximum	167.72	187.55

The One That Wasn't Produced
1984 & 1986

The March-April 1984 issue of the *Successful Dealer*, a newsletter for the WFE dealers, included a paragraph about projects being developed by the WFE engineering department. These projects included a 6-cylinder engine for the 2-180 and a higher horsepower four-wheel-drive tractor which was identified as the 4-325. In 1986 after the purchase of the company by Allied Products, the 4-325 was again mentioned in an interview with Mr. Terry, the president of White.

The 6-cylinder engine for the 2-180 appeared as the Field Boss 185. The one that didn't make it to production was the 4-325.

The 4-325 was an experimental four-wheel-drive tractor which used the basic articulated frame of the 4-270, but with a longer

The experimental WFE 4-325 on display in Charles City, Iowa, in July 1996.

front frame for the larger engine with an additional 55 horsepower. The power plant was a Caterpillar 3406 6-cylinder engine equipped with a turbocharger and aftercooler. It had a 893-cubic-inch displacement resulting from a 5.4- x 6.5-inch bore and stroke. Also there were wider gears in the transmission for the increased loads. If the 4-325 had gone into production, there were plans to revise the gear ratios to further reduce the torque loads in the transmission.

Three prototypes were built with one being used for dynamometer and hydraulic tests and two for field work. One of the prototypes has survived and is being used on a farm near Charles City, Iowa. However, the original Caterpillar engine was removed for teardown and evaluation after the test work was completed and this 4-325 is now equipped with a Caterpillar engine which is normally used in truck applications.

The End of an Era
1988-1995

Early in 1988 White-New Idea announced plans to relocate the assembly and painting of the White line of tractors to their plant in Coldwater, Ohio. The last tractor assembled at Charles City was a White 100 on March 25, 1988. On June 6, 1988, White started building tractors on its new assembly line in Coldwater. And thus ended an era which had started with the assembly of Hart-Parr No. 1 in late 1901 or early 1902.

The Charles City plant continued to function as a foundry and machining operation until Allied Products closed it on July 31, 1993. A week-long auction was held in October 1993 to completely liquidate all the equipment in the plant. Demolition of the factory buildings began in November 1994 and all that remains today is a large concrete slab.

Spirit of Oliver
1988

During the 1988 fall farm shows, White-New Idea exhibited a prototype tractor which was named the Spirit of Oliver. It was built from a White 185 with a Power Front Axle, but was painted Oliver green with gold and white trim and accented with a chrome muffler and wheel rims. The cab interior was restyled with a wood dash and console. Plans to build a limited run were cancelled after the 1988 drought caused the agricultural economy to deteriorate.

A second Spirit of Oliver was built for the 1990 exhibit season along with a Spirit of MM and a Spirit of Cockshutt. These tractors were White 140 tractors painted three different colors with extra trim and lettering to emphasize the heritage of the White tractor line. Both Spirit of Oliver tractors were sold to farmers in Ohio.

The Spirit of Oliver tractor was used to survey farmers at the 1988 farm shows about their ideas for future tractor features.

White American 60 & 80
1989-1991

As a result of the survey conducted of the viewers of the Spirit of Oliver, White-New Idea introduced two new tractor models in February 1989 which were available in four colors — White silver, Oliver green, Minneapolis-Moline gold, and Cockshutt red. The other unique feature of these 60- and 80-PTO horsepower tractors was they were the only tractors of this size being assembled in the United States, so they were named the American 60 and the American 80. The styling was similar to the Spirit of Oliver with the grill positioned below the hood and extending along the sides of the tractor for a short distance. The headlights were built into the front of the hood. The 60 and 80 replaced the 2-55, 2-65, and 2-75 which were built by Iseki.

The program to design and build a line of tractors in the tradition of the Oliver 1550 started in May 1987. The new models included the traditional cast-iron frame for weight and rigidity. Both provided the choice of an adjustable front axle or a front-wheel drive with a limited slip differential. After the first year, an extra-wide adjustable front axle was made available for use in vegetable fields and a semi-high clearance front axle with 28 inches of crop clearance was provided for speciality crops.

Both models used 239-cubic-inch, 4-cylinder CDC-Cummins diesel engines. The engine for the 60 was naturally aspirated and the 80 was equipped with the tur-

The two American series models were available in green, gold, red, and silver colors to promote their heritage.

bocharged version. The displacement for the 4-cylinder engine was 67 percent of the 359-cubic-inch, 6-cylinder engine used in the 100, 120, and 140 models because the bore and stroke were the same. The standard transmission, with the gear shift lever in the middle of the floor, provided six forward speeds and two in reverse, but a 3-speed powershift package could be added which tripled the number of speeds in both directions.

The operator's station provided a flat platform, a deluxe adjustable seat, and a 2-post ROPS. The console at the right of the seat contained the throttle, powershift, PTO, and hydraulic controls. Power steering was standard. After the first year, a cab with a ROPS-type frame and a three-sided front became available for the 60 and 80. It was isolated from the rest of the tractor and featured a tilting-type steering wheel.

The independent PTO for both models was engaged with a modulated wet multi-disk clutch. The 60 had the 540-rpm type as standard and the dual speed 540/1,000-rpm unit was available as an option. The 80 was equipped with the dual speed unit as standard equipment. Both models used an open center hydraulic system to power the Category 2 size of 3-point hitch. One set of remote outlets was standard and the second and third sets were optional.

The performance of the American 60 and American 80 models was measured at the Nebraska Tractor Test Lab in April 1990 with the following results:

The American 60 and 80 were powered with a CDC-Cummins engine, but the 80's engine was turbocharged.

Model	Test No.	Type of Test	Drawbar Hp	PTO Hp
White American 60 Diesel	1636	Maximum	52.39	61.07
White American 80 Diesel	1637	Maximum	71.01	81.48

White 125, 145, 170, & 195
1990-1992

The Workhorse tractor models were introduced as "new for 1991" with the 125, 145, 170, and 195 replacing the 120, 140, 160, and 185 models. The 100 was dropped without a replacement. The general configuration, including the cab with the three-sided front, did not change, but the stripe on the sides of the hood was redesigned to a more graphic design. It had a red outline and black stripes at the front changing into a black background at the rear for the model number and the figure of a horse. The emphasis was on the power and fuel economy of the Cummins engines coupled with the 18-speed transmission.

The new models improved the the operator's comfort. The wheel base with the PosiTrac Power Front Axle was lengthened from 90 to 102 inches for the 170 and 195 for a better ride, while it remained at 99 inches for the 125 and 145 models. New angled steps and a relocated door latch made it easier to enter the cab. The deluxe air ride seat, which was orthopedically designed for excellent support, was now standard equipment. The air cleaner intake was placed under the hood for improved visibility. Optional equipment included four additional halogen flood lights which mounted to the cab roof, an insulated storage compartment to keep food hot or cold, and a quick hitch for attaching 3-point hitch implements.

The power plants for the four new models did not change as the 125 and 145 used two versions of the 359-cubic-inch CDC-Cummins engine and the

By 1990 the typical large two-wheel-drive tractor was equipped with a cab, dual rear wheels, and a front-wheel drive.

Just as the power increased to pull larger implements, the lift capacity of the 3-point hitch was increased to lift these larger implements.

170 and 195 was equipped with two versions of the 505-cubic-inch CDC-Cummins engine. All four engines were turbocharged and the engines used in the 145 and 195 were also aftercooled. The transmission continued to provide 18 forward speeds with three powershift speeds in each of six gears.

The new models appeared to have slightly more power than the previous ones, but it was a different selection of data from the same Nebraska Tractor Tests. The previous models listed the maximum PTO horsepower at rated engine speed. The new models listed the power output with the torque rise at reduced engine speed, as illustrated below:

Previous Tractor Model	PTO Hp at Rated Speed	Advertised % Torque Rise	New Tractor Model	PTO Hp at Reduced Speed
120	119.13	27	125	121.94
140	138.53	26	145	140.30
160	162.47	30	170	165.97
185	187.55	31	195	192.38

The PTO was the independent type and provided 540- and 1,000-rpm speeds for the 125 and 145. The more powerful 170 and 195 were equipped with a 1,000-rpm PTO. The closed center hydraulic system provided a 3-point hitch lift capacity of 7,200 pounds for the 125 and 145 and 8,500 pounds for the 170 and 195. An optional boost package increased the lift capacity to 8,540 pounds for the two smaller models and to 9,900 pounds for the two larger models.

Since the engines and transmissions did not change, the White 125, 145, 170, and 195 models were not tested at Nebraska. Instead they used the results of Tests 1615, 1616, 1607, and 1608.

The AGCO White Models

AGCO White 6065, 6085, & 6105
1992-Current

In June 1991 the Deutz-Allis Corporation purchased the White tractor line from the Allied Products Corporation and moved the production from Coldwater, Ohio, to Independence, Missouri. This acquisition meant Deutz-Allis would no longer be purchasing its larger models from White-New Idea, but instead would be the manufacturer of both the Deutz-Allis and White tractors. As a result, the corporate name was changed to Allis Gleaner Company (AGCO) and Deutz-Allis remained as a brand name.

The first new White tractor models introduced by AGCO were the 6065 with 62 PTO horsepower, the 6085 with 80 PTO horsepower, and the 6105 with 106 PTO horsepower. These three models were introduced to the dealers in February 1992 and replaced the American 60 and 80 models. The tractors were manufactured in Italy by S + L + H S.p.A., the company that manufactured the SAME, Lamborghini, and Hurlimann tractors. They were painted the traditional White silver with a black chassis. This time the hood stripe was red and black.

The 6065 and 6085 were available in four configurations with a choice of the

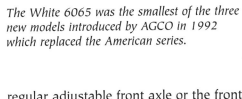

The White 6065 was the smallest of the three new models introduced by AGCO in 1992 which replaced the American series.

regular adjustable front axle or the front-wheel drive plus the choice of a ROPS or a cab. Since the cab was standard for the 6105, its configuration was limited to the two choices for the front axle. The cab had a flat platform, a ROPS frame, and two doors plus a roof hatch.

The power plants were Lamborghini liquid cooled diesel engines, all with a 4.14- x 4.55-inch bore and stroke. The 4-cylinder engine for the 6065 had a 244-cubic-inch displacement and was naturally aspirated. The 6085 was powered with a turbocharged version of the same 4-cylinder engine. The 6105 was equipped with a 6-cylinder, naturally aspirated version, so its displacement was 366 cubic inches.

The 6065 and 6085 provided 12 forward speeds and 12 in reverse. They used a 4-speed synchronized transmission with a 3-speed range selector and a synchronized forward/reverse shuttle. A creeper transmission with 16 speeds in both directions was optional, but later became the standard transmission for the 6085. The standard transmission for the 6105 used the same arrangement, but with a 6-speed transmission and a 4-speed range selector for 24 forward speeds and 12 in reverse. Its optional transmission provided 36 speeds in each direction by using a 6-speed transmission, a 3-speed range selection with a reverse, and a 2-speed rear axle.

All three models were equipped with an independent 540-/1,000-rpm PTO. The 6065 cab version, the 6085, and 6105 were equipped with an economy PTO setting for light PTO loads which provided the proper PTO speed at an engine speed reduction of 25 percent. The open center hydraulic system operated the Category 2 size of 3-point hitch.

The three models were tested in Italy in 1987 and 1991 and the Nebraska Summary Reports listed the following results:

Model	Test No.	Type of Test	Drawbar Hp	PTO Hp
AGCO White 6065 Diesel	108	Maximum	54.53	62.77
AGCO White 6085 Diesel	110	Maximum	68.62	80.15
AGCO White 6105 Diesel	111	Maximum	88.28	106.3

The cab was standard equipment for the White 6105, but the front-wheel drive was optional.

Shipments of four new models of AGCO White tractors began early in 1993 from the factory in Independence, Missouri. Although these new row-crop models retained the traditional silver color, they had their first major styling change since 1975. Styled to match the mid-size models, the wider hood, grill, and partial engine side panels appeared to be one piece. The air cleaner was under the hood and the exhaust stack was relocated to the right side of the cab for an unobstructed view over the hood.

AGCO White 6125, 6145, 6175, & 6195
1993-Current

The 6125 was initially rated at 121 PTO horsepower at rated engine speed and the 6145 had a rating of 140 horsepower. The 6175 was rated at 166 PTO horsepower and the 6195 at 192 horsepower. The four new models replaced the 125, 145, 170, and 195 models.

The new feature of these four models, which the first owners ranked at the top of their list, was the 18-speed powershift transmission. Unlike the previous 18-speed transmissions in Oliver and White tractors, this one was a full powershift with the ability to move to any of the 18 speeds without using the clutch. The 18 speeds ranged from about 1.5 to 24 mph for the four models.

The completely new cab provided a smoother ride with the operator positioned 15 inches forward and 2 inches higher than in the previous models. This cab had a wide, flat windshield which joined with the side windows at the front corners

The White 6100 series with its sloping hood and rounded outline featured the first major styling change for White tractors since 1975.

without a corner post. The deluxe air-ride seat could swivel 10 degrees to the right and 20 degrees to the left. A new, unique feature was the powershift console which was attached to the seat, immediately ahead of the right arm rest. This small console contained the throttle and shift levers plus rocker switches for the front-wheel drive and differential lock. The main console was located on the right side of the cab and contained the other control levers. The powershift display was located on the right front cab post and the other instrumentation was on the dash. A buddy seat, with a seat belt, was located on the left side of the cab.

Three of the major components remained unchanged. The tractors continued to be built around a cast-iron frame which provided rigidity and weight at the front of the tractor. The front-wheel drive was optional for the 6125, 6145, and 6175, but was standard for the 6195 model. The power plants continued to be the turbocharged CDC-Cummins diesel engines with the ones for the 6145 and 6195 also being aftercooled. The engine displacement was 359 cubic inches for the 6125 and 6145 and 505 cubic inches for the 6175 and 6195.

The PTO remained the dual speed type for the 6125 and 6145 and the 1,000-rpm type for the two larger models. The closed center hydraulic system continued to provide a 3-point hitch lift capacity of 7,200 pounds for the 6125 and 6145, 8,500 pounds for the 6175, but the 9,900 pounds capacity was now standard for the 6195. An optional 3-point hitch stepped the capacity of the 6125 and 6145 up to 8,540 pounds and the 6175 up to 9,900 pounds.

The 6125 and 6145 were tested at Nebraska in May 1994 and the 6175 and 6195 in October 1994. The results of the tests at the rated engine speed of 2,200 rpm were:

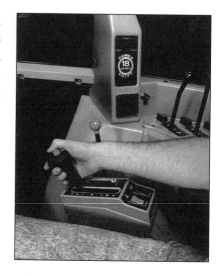

The 18-speed full powershift transmission was controlled with a lever mounted in a small console attached to the right arm rest.

Model	Test No.	Type of Test	Drawbar Hp	PTO Hp
AGCO White 6125 Diesel	148	Maximum	112.08	124.94
AGCO White 6145 Diesel	149	Maximum	127.65	142.70
AGCO White 6175 Diesel	169	Maximum	154.72	175.47
AGCO White 6195 Diesel	170	Maximum	174.70	200.46

AGCO White 6124, 6144, & 6215
1995-Current

At the June 1994 dealer meeting, White introduced three "new for 1995" tractor models. The new 6215 was the largest row-crop tractor ever built by Oliver or White. It was similar to the 6175 and 6195, but produced 215 PTO horsepower with its 505-cubic-inch CDC-Cummins engine which had a wastegate turbocharger and an aftercooler. Standard equipment included a full powershift transmission with 18 forward speeds, a front-wheel drive, and the cab. The 3-point hitch lifted 14,000 pounds.

The new 6124 and 6144 were versions of the 6125 and 6145 models. The 124-PTO horsepower 6124 and the 144-PTO horsepower 6144 were equipped with a more economical 32-speed partial powershift transmission. The new trans-

The White 6124 and 6144 featured a more economical 32-speed partial powershift transmission.

mission used an 8-speed gear box in combination with a 4-speed powershift and a forward/reverse shuttle to provide 32 speeds in both directions. Also the 3-point hitch provided a larger lifting capacity of 10,400 pounds.

AGCO White 6045
1996-Current

The White 6045 low-profile utility tractor which was rated at 45 PTO horsepower was "new for 1996." It was built by S + L + H, had the same styling as the other utility tractors, and could be equipped with an adjustable front axle or a front-wheel drive. A 2-post ROPS was standard.

The 6045 was powered with a 3-cylinder version of the 4-cylinder diesel engine used by the 6065. The standard transmission had 12 speeds in both directions and the optional one had 16 speeds forward and 8 in reverse. Both transmissions featured a synchronized shuttle.

AGCO introduced two AGCOSTAR models for selected AGCO Allis and AGCO White dealers in the autumn of 1995 as "new for 1996." These restyled four-wheel-drive tractors traced their roots back to the Massey Ferguson articulated models and more recently to the McConnell Marc 900 and

AGCOSTAR 8360 & 8425
1995-Current

1000 tractors. The two models were painted the White silver color and were built in the former White-New Idea factory in Coldwater, Ohio, which AGCO acquired in late 1993.

The ROPS type of cab for this four-wheel-drive tractor featured an isolation mounting and a insulated interior to reduce the sound level. Other features for the comfort of the operator included tinted glass, a tilt and telescoping steering wheel, a deluxe air-ride seat, and a convenient right side console. The hood sloped down and the muffler was located near the right front corner of the cab to improve forward visibility.

The 8360 was available with a 360-horsepower Cummins N14 6-cylinder diesel engine. The second model, the 8425, was equipped with a 425-horsepower engine, either the 855-cubic-inch Cummins N14 series or the 744-cubic-inch Detroit Diesel Series 60. Both engines were equipped with electronic monitors to increase fuel economy and reduce operating costs. The engines were combined with an Eaton-Fuller constant mesh transmission with 18 forward speeds and 2 reverse speeds.

Besides the engines, the only other option was the wheels and tires. The two models could be equipped with a variety of dual and triple combinations.

Two lights in the grill, four across the front of the cab, and more aimed to the rear provided visibility for working at night.

Appendix

Nebraska Tractor Test Results
1920-1996

Before the Nebraska Tractor Tests started in 1920, there was a wide variation in how the various companies rated their tractors. As a result, universities began to conduct comparison tests. Listed below is a table of results of the Tractor Tests conducted at Ohio State University in January 1919. This table was taken from a Hart-Parr publication which

explains why the Hart-Parr 30 tractor is listed at the top in bold print. Notice the differences between the rated belt horsepower in column 2 and the test results in column 6 for the various makes.

The following results from the Nebraska Tractor Tests lists the observed maximum belt or PTO horsepower at rated engine speed. This data is available for every tractor tested at Nebraska and is the power level most often used by manufacturers today. It will be more than the "rated" values used in the 1920s and 1930s, but less than the "corrected" values which were used from 1936 through 1958.

Tractor Test at Ohio State University
January 27-31, 1919

Name of Tractor in Test	RATING Draw Bar	Belt	Number of Cylinders	Fuel Used	Price	TEST RESULTS Horse Power	Fuel Cost per HP. hr.
HART-PARR		**30**	**2**	**Kerosene**	**$1395**	**37.5**	**.01504**
I. H. C.	15	30	4	Kerosene	$2000	35	.0216
Aultman Taylor	15	30	4	Kerosene	2300	33.4	.02212
Wallis Cub	15	25	4	Gasoline	1600	31.8	.0285
Russell	20	40	4	Kerosene	3000	31.6	.0254
Moline	9	18	4	Gasoline	1575	28.7	.0373
Huber	12	25	4	Kerosene	1385	28.3	.01952
Case	15	27	4	Kerosene	1600	27.7	.0166
Rumely	12	20	2	Kerosene	1700	25.5	.0154
Emerson	12	20	4	Kerosene	1455	24.7	.0219
Frick	12	25	4	Kerosene	1650	24.5	.01633
Titan	10	20	2	Kerosene	1260	24.1	.01504
Steel Mule	12	20	4	Kerosene	1875	21.4	.0183
Fordson	11	22	4	Kerosene	895	21.4	.0177
Waterloo Boy	12	25	2	Kerosene	1350	21.2	.01581
Case	10	18	4	Kerosene	1200	19.8	.0173
Elgin	12	25	4	Kerosene	1385	19.2	.0159
Cleveland	12	20	4	Gasoline	1585	19.2	.0392
Shelby	9	18	4	Gasoline	1250	18.6	.04936
Avery	12	25	2	Kerosene	1270	18.3	.0178
Port Huron	12	25	4	Kerosene	1600	14.4	.03438
Avery	8	16	2	Withdrawn			

This is the only Tractor Test held to date in 1919.

Year	Test No.	Model	Fuel	Obsrv. Max. Belt Hp	Cyl.- Displ. (cu. in.)	Rated Engine Speed (rpm)
Hart-Parr						
1921	79	10-20 B	Kero	23.01	2 - 281	800
1920	26	15-30 A	Kero	31.37	2 - 464	750
1923	97	22-40	Kero	46.40	4 - 616	800
1924	107	12-24 E	Kero	26.97	2 - 308	800
1924	106	16-30 E	Kero	37.03	2 - 464	750
1926	129	12-24 G	Dist	31.99	2 - 337	850
1926	128	18-36 G	Dist	42.85	2 - 500	800
1927	140	28-50	Dist	64.56	4 - 674	850
Oliver Hart-Parr						
1930	176	18-27 R.C.	Kero	29.72	4 - 280	1,150
1930	180	18-28	Kero	30.29	4 - 280	1,190
1930	183	28-44	Kero	49.04	4 - 443	1,125
1936	252	Row Crop 70	Gas	28.40	6 - 201	1,500
1936	267	Row Crop 70	Dist	27.15	6 - 201	1,500
1937	283	Standard 70	Gas	27.79	6 - 201	1,500
1937	284	Standard 70	Dist	26.75	6 - 201	1,500
Oliver						
1938	300	Row Crop 80	Dist	38.78	4 - 334	1,200
1938	301	Standard 80	Dist	39.32	4 - 334	1,200
1940	365	Standard 80	Gas	41.27	4 - 298	1,200

Year	Test No.	Model	Fuel	Obsrv. Max. Belt Hp	Cyl.-Displ. (cu. in.)	Rated Engine Speed (rpm)
1940	351	Row Crop 70	Gas	31.52	6 - 201	1,500
1941	375	Row Crop 60	Gas	18.76	4 - 120	1,500
1947	388	Row Crop 88	Gas	41.99	6 - 231	1,600
1947-48	391	Standard 88	Gas	43.15	6 - 231	1,600
1948	404	Row Crop 77	Gas	33.98	6 - 194	1,600
1948	405	Standard 77	Gas	33.56	6 - 194	1,600
1949	412	Row Crop 66	Gas	24.91	4 - 129	1,600
1949	413	Standard 66	Gas	24.90	4 - 129	1,600
1949	425	Row Crop 77	Gas	37.17	6 - 194	1,600
1949	434	HG Crawler	Gas	25.30	4 - 133	1,700
1950	451	99 (Standard)	Gas	62.28	4 - 443	1,125
1950	450	Row Crop 88	Diesel	43.53	6 - 231	1,600
1951	457	Row Crop 77	Diesel	35.79	6 - 194	1,600
1951	467	Row Crop 66	Diesel	25.03	4 - 129	1,600
1952	470	Row Crop 77	LP-gas	36.33	6 - 194	1,600
1954	516	OC-6 Crawler	Gas	No test	6 - 194	1,600
1954	517	OC-6 Crawler	Diesel	No test	6 - 194	1,600
1954	524	Super 55	Gas	34.39	4 - 144	2,000
1954	526	Super 55	Diesel	33.71	4 - 144	2,000
1955	541	Super 66	Gas	33.62	4 - 144	2,000
1955	544	Super 66	Diesel	33.69	4 - 144	2,000
1955	542	Super 77	Gas	43.98	6 - 216	1,600
1955	543	Super 77	Diesel	44.05	6 - 216	1,600
1954	525	Super 88	Gas	55.77	6 - 265	1,600
1954	527	Super 88	Diesel	54.88	6 - 265	1,600
1955	557	Super 99	Diesel	62.39	6 - 302	1,675
1955	556	Super 99 GM	Diesel	78.74	3 - 213*	1,675
1958	648	770	Gas	50.04	6 - 216	1,750
1958	649	770	Diesel	48.80	6 - 216	1,750
1958	647	880	Gas	61.86	6 - 265	1,750
1958	650	880	Diesel	59.48	6 - 265	1,750
1958	660	950	Diesel	67.23	6 - 302	1,800
1958	661	990 GM	Diesel	84.10	3 - 213*	1,800
1958	662	995 GM Lugmatic	Diesel	85.37	3 - 213*	2,000

Year	Test No.	Model	Fuel	Obsrv. Max. PTO Hp	Cyl.-Displ. (cu. in.)†	Rated Engine Speed (rpm)
1960	735	500 (DB 850)	Gas	32.00	4 - 154	2,000
1960	734	500 (DB 850)	Diesel	33.56	4 - 154	2,000
1959	697	550	Gas	41.39	4 - 155	2,000
1959	698	550	Diesel	39.21	4 - 155	2,000
1965	903	600 (DB 990)	Diesel	51.60	4 - 186	2,200
1960	766	1800	Gas	73.92	6 - 265	2,000
1960	767	1800	Diesel	70.15	6 - 283	2,000
1960	768	1900	Diesel	89.35	4 - 212*	2,000
1962	824	1900 B	Diesel	98.54	4 - 212*	2,200
1963	847	1900 B w/fwd	Diesel	100.62	4 - 212*	2,200
1962	831	1800 B	Diesel	77.04	6 - 310	2,200
1962	832	1800 B w/fwd	Diesel	76.97	6 - 310	2,200
1963	839	1800 B	Gas	80.16	6 - 283	2,200
1963	846	1800 B w/fwd	Gas	80.72	6 - 283	2,200
1963	840	1600	Diesel	57.95	6 - 265	1,900
1963	841	1600	Gas	56.50	6 - 231	1,900
1964	871	1950	Diesel	105.79	4 - 212*	2,400
1964	872	1950 w/fwd	Diesel	105.78	4 - 212*	2,400
1964	870	1850	Diesel	92.94	6 - 354	2,400
1964	869	1850 w/fwd	Diesel	92.92	6 - 354	2,400
1964	875	1850	Gas	92.43	6 - 310	2,400
1964	876	1850 w/fwd	Gas	92.92	6 - 310	2,400
1964	873	1650	Diesel	66.28	6 - 283	2,200
1964	874	1650	Gas	66.72	6 - 265	2,200
1966	943	1550	Diesel	53.50	6 - 232	2,200
1966	944	1550	Gas	53.34	6 - 232	2,200
1967	962	1750	Diesel	80.05	6 - 310	2,400
1967	961	1750	Gas	80.31	6 - 283	2,400
1967	969	1950-T	Diesel	105.24	6 - 310 T	2,400
1968	972	1950-T w/fwd	Diesel	105.11	6 - 310 T	2,400
1968	987	2050	Diesel	118.78	6 - 478	2,400
1968	986	2150	Diesel	131.48	6 - 478 T	2,400

* 2-cycle engine.
† T is turbocharged; T&I is turbocharged and intercooled.

Year	Test No.	Model	Fuel	Obsrv. Max. PTO Hp	Cyl.-Displ. (cu. in.)†	Rated Engine Speed (rpm)
1970	1041	1655	Diesel	70.57	6 - 283	2,200
1970	1042	1655	Gas	70.27	6 - 265	2,200
1970	1057	1755	Diesel	86.93	6 - 310	2,400
1970	1056	1755	Gas	86.98	6 - 283	2,400
1970	1040	1855	Diesel	98.60	6 - 310 T	2,400
1970	1055	1955	Diesel	108.16	6 - 310 T	2,400
1968	978	1865 (MM G900)	Diesel	97.78	6 - 451	1,800
1968	979	1865 (MM G900)	LP-gas	97.57	6 - 425	1,800
1966	953	2055 (MM G1000)	Diesel	110.78	6 - 504	1,800
1966	954	2055 (MM G1000)	LP-gas	110.76	6 - 504	1,800
1971	1069	2155 (MM G1350)	Diesel	141.44	6 - 585	2,200
1973	1140	2255	Diesel	146.72	V-8 - 573	2,600
1971	1070	2655 (MM 4WD)	Diesel	143.27	6 - 585	2,200

White Field Boss

Year	Test No.	Model	Fuel	Obsrv. Max. PTO Hp	Cyl.-Displ. (cu. in.)†	Rated Engine Speed (rpm)
1975	1184	4-180	Diesel	181.07	V-8 - 636	2,800
1974	1159	4-150	Diesel	151.87	V-8 - 636	2,800
1975	1182	2-150	Diesel	147.49	6 - 585	2,200
1975	1181	2-105	Diesel	105.61	6 - 354 T	2,200
1976	1213	2-85	Diesel	85.54	6 - 354	2,200
1976	1212	2-70	Diesel	70.71	6 - 283	2,200
1977	1232	2-60	Diesel	63.22	4 - 211	2,400
1977	1231	2-50	Diesel	47.02	3 - 158	2,500
1978	1275	2-135	Diesel	137.64	6 - 478 T	2,200
1978	1276	2-155	Diesel	157.73	6 - 478 T	2,200
1978	1287	2-180	Diesel	181.89	V-8 - 636	2,800
1980	1375	4-175	Diesel	151.69	V-8 - 636	2,600
1979	1318	4-210	Diesel	182.44	V-8 - 636	2,800
1980	1373	2-30	Diesel	28.33	3 - 91	2,600
1980	1374	2-35	Diesel	32.84	3 - 108	2,400
1981	1395	2-45	Diesel	43.73	4 - 169	2,250
1981	1396	2-62	Diesel	61.46	4 - 219	2,200
1983	1466	2-55	Diesel	53.32	4 - 199	2,200
1983	1467	2-65	Diesel	62.50	4 - 235	2,200

Year	Test No.	Model	Fuel	Obsrv. Max. PTO Hp	Cyl.-Displ. (cu. in.)†	Rated Engine Speed (rpm)
1983	1486	2-75	Diesel	75.39	6 - 329	2,200
1983	1487	2-88	Diesel	86.78	6 - 354	2,200
1983	1468	2-110	Diesel	110.52	6 - 354 T	2,200
1985	1558	4-225	Diesel	195.65	V-8 - 636 T	2,600
1985	1559	4-270	Diesel	239.25	6 - 638 T&I	2,100

White

Year	Test No.	Model	Fuel	Obsrv. Max. PTO Hp	Cyl.-Displ. (cu. in.)†	Rated Engine Speed (rpm)
1988	1608	185	Diesel	187.55	6 - 505 T&I	2,200
1988	1607	160	Diesel	162.47	6 - 505 T	2,200
1988	1616	140	Diesel	138.53	6 - 359 T&I	2,200
1988	1615	120	Diesel	119.13	6 - 359 T	2,200
1988	1614	100	Diesel	94.36	6 - 359	2,400
1990	1637	80	Diesel	81.48	4 - 239 T	2,200
1990	1636	60	Diesel	61.07	4 - 239	2,200

AGCO White

Year	Test No.	Model	Fuel	Obsrv. Max. PTO Hp	Cyl.-Displ. (cu. in.)†	Rated Engine Speed (rpm)
1987	108	6065	Diesel	62.77	4 - 244	2,350
1987	110	6085	Diesel	80.15	4 - 244 T	2,500
1991	111	6105	Diesel	106.3	6 - 366	2,500
1994	148	6125	Diesel	124.94	6 - 359 T	2,200
1994	149	6145	Diesel	142.70	6 - 359 T&I	2,200
1994	169	6175	Diesel	175.47	6 - 505 T	2,200
1994	170	6195	Diesel	200.46	6 - 505 T&I	2,200
1995	180	6124	Diesel	124.94	6 - 359 T	2,200
1995	181	6144	Diesel	142.56	6 - 359 T&I	2,200
1996	214	6215	Diesel	215.44	6 - 505 T&I	2,200

AGCOSTAR

Year	Test No.	Model	Fuel	Obsrv. Max. PTO Hp	Cyl.-Displ. (cu. in.)†	Rated Engine Speed (rpm)
1996	215	8360 (4WD)	Diesel	326.62‡	6 - 855 T&I	2,100
1996	216	8425 (4WD)	Diesel	396.34‡	6 - 855 T&I	2,100

† T is turbocharged; T&I is turbocharged and intercooled.
‡ Measured at the transfer case output shaft.

Hart-Parr, Oliver, and White Serial Numbers

1901-1991

Recognition and praise must be given to Doug Strawser who has painstakingly searched every record, list, catalog, and ledger that can be found to compile the serial number information for wheel type tractors for the years 1901-1954. The following listing for 1901-1954 is a summary of the information Strawser presented at the February 1994 meeting of the Hart-Parr/Oliver Collectors Association. The serial numbers for wheel type tractors after 1954 and the crawler tractors are from information at the Floyd County Museum.

Hart-Parr

Model 17-30
1901/02	Described as No. 1
1902	Described as No. 2
1903	1 206 - 1 219
1904	1 339 - 1 340
1905	1 346 - 1 347
	1 420 & 1 422
1906	1 435 - 1 444
	1 446 - 1 454

Model 22-40
1903	1 222 - 1 245
1904	1 306 - 1 338
	1 341 - 1 345
1905	1 364 - 1 388
	1 390 - 1 393

1905	1 415 - 1 419
	1 421
	1 423 - 1 434
1906	1 445
	1 455 - 1 604
1907	1 605 - 1 810

Model 22-45
1908	1 811 - 2 014
1909	2 025 - 2 324
1910	2 432 - 3 310
1911	3 311 - 3 811

Model 30-60
1911	3 812 - 4 111
	4 212 - 4 300
1912	4 301 - 4 711
	4 814 - 4 913
1913	4 916 - 5 415
1914	5 416 - 5 480
1915	5 481 - 5 674
1916	5 675 - 5 715

Model 40-80
1908	2 015 - 2 018
1909	2 019 - 2 024

Model 15-30 (Horizontal Cylinders)
1909	2 325 - 2 331
	(Recalled)

Model 15-30 (Vertical Cylinders)
1910	2 332 - 2 403
1911	2 404 - 2 431

Model 20-40 (Vertical Cylinders)
1911	4 112 - 4 211
1912	4 714 - 4 736
1913	4 737 - 4 793
1914	4 794 - 4 813

Model 12-27
1913	5 816 - 5 934
1914	5 935 - 6 039

Model 18-35
1914	6 040 - 6 063
1915	6 064 - 6 153
1916	6 154 - 6 199
1917	6 200 - 6 215
	8 201 - 8 358
1918	8 359 - 8 400
1919	20 001 - 20 050

Little Devil (15-22)
1914	6 219 - 6 244
1915	6 245 - 6 743
1916	6 744 - 6 943

New Hart-Parr (12-25) & Model 30 (15-30 A)
1918	8 401 - 9 001
	9 201 - 9 382
1919	9 383 - 13 017
1920	13 018 - 14 198
	15 550 - 18 474
1921	18 475 - 18 841
1922	18 842 - 19 125

Model 30 (15-30 C)
1922	21 001 - 21 392
1923	21 393 - 21 864

1924	21 865 - 22 300

Model 16-30 E
1924	22 501 - 22 600
1925	22 601 - 24 000

Model 16-30 F
1926	24 001 - 26 000

Model 18-36 G
1926	26 001 - 26 361
1927	26 362 - 28 850

Model 18-36 H
1927	28 851 - 29 635
1928	29 636 - 33 752

Model 18-36 I
1928	33 753 - 34 566
1929	34 567 - 35 000
	85 001 - 89 159
1930	89 160 - 90 698

Model 20 (10-20 B)
1920	35 001 - 35 024
1921	35 025 - 35 199
1922	35 200 - 35 319

Model 20 (10-20 C)
1922	35 501 - 35 521
1923	35 522 - 35 749
1924	35 750 - 35 922

Model 12-24 E
1924	36 001 - 36 074
1925	36 075 - 36 580
1926	36 581 - 37 100

Model 12-24 G
| 1926 | 37 101 - 37 189 |
| 1927 | 37 190 - 37 900 |

Model 12-24 H
1927	37 901 - 38 118
1928	38 119 - 39 686
1929	39 687 - 42 278
1930	42 279 - 43 253

Model 40 (22-40)
1923	70 001 - 70 019
1924	70 020 - 70 094
1925	70 095 - 70 250
1926	70 251 - 70 490
1927	70 491 - 70 500

Model 28-50 (narrow radiator)
| 1927 | 70 501 - 70 741 |
| 1928 | 70 742 - 70 951 |

Model 28-50 (wide radiator)
1928	70 952 - 70 967
1929	70 968 - 71 401
1930	71 402 - 71 701

Oliver Hart-Parr

Row Crop 18-27
(single front wheel)
| 1930 | 100 001 - 102 648 |
| 1931 | 102 649 - 103 300 |

Row Crop 18-27
(dual front wheels)
1931	103 301 - 103 318
1932	103 319 - 103 617
1933	103 618 - 104 038
1934	104 039 - 104 850
1935	104 851 - 107 311
1936	107 312 - 108 573
1937	108 574 - 109 151

Model 18-28
1930	800 001 - 800 459
1931	800 460 - 800 963
1932	800 964 - 800 984
1933	800 985 - 801 050
1934	801 051 - 801 240
1935	801 241 - 801 989
1936	801 990 - 802 937
1937	802 938 - 803 928

Model 28-44
1930	500 001 - 503 599
1931	503 600 - 506 184
1932	506 185 - 506 211
1933	506 212 - 506 254
1934	506 255 - 506 400
1935	506 401 - 507 175

Model 28-44 &
High Compression Special
| 1936 | 507 176 - 508 015 |
| 1937 | 508 016 - 508 917 |

Row Crop 70
(Oliver Hart-Parr style)
1935	200 001 - 200 685
1936	200 686 - 208 728
1937	208 729 - 216 925

Standard 70
(Oliver Hart-Parr style)
| 1936 | 300 001 - 300 633 |
| 1937 | 300 634 - 301 802 |

Oliver

Row Crop 60 (4-speed)
1940	600 001 - 600 070
1941	600 071 - 606 303
1942	606 304 - 607 394
1943	607 395 - 608 525
1944	608 526 - 609 930

Row Crop 60 (5-speed)
1944	609 931 - 612 046
1945	612 047 - 615 627
1946	615 628 - 616 706
1947	616 707 - 620 256
1948	620 257 - 625 131

Standard 60 (4-speed)
| 1942 | 410 001 - 410 500 |
| 1943 | 410 501 - 410 510 |

Standard 60 (5-speed)
1944	410 511 - 410 616
1945	410 617 - 410 910
1946	410 911 - 411 310
1947	411 311 - 411 960
1948	411 961 - 413 605

Row Crop 70 (4-speed std.)
1937	216 926 - 219 644
	220 426 - 220 694
1938	219 645 - 220 425
	220 695 - 223 254
1939	223 255 - 231 115
1940	231 116 - 236 355
1941	236 356 - 241 390
1942	241 391 - 243 639
1943	243 640 - 244 710
1944	244 711 - 245 040

Row Crop 70 (6-speed std.)
1944	245 041 - 250 179
1945	250 180 - 252 779
1946	252 780 - 258 139
1947	258 140 - 262 839
1948	262 840 - 267 866

Standard 70 (4-speed std.)
1937	301 803 - 302 083
1938	302 084 - 303 464
1939	303 465 - 305 361
1940	305 362 - 306 593
1941	306 594 - 307 579

| 1942 | 307 580 - 308 187 |
| 1943 | 308 188 - 308 483 |

Standard 70 (6-speed std.)
1944	308 484 - 310 217
1945	310 218 - 311 115
1946	311 116 - 312 689
1947	312 690 - 314 220
1948	314 221 - 315 420

Row Crop 80 (3-speed)
1937	109 152 - 109 166
1938	109 167 - 109 782
1939	109 783 - 109 852

Row Crop 80 (4-speed)
1939	109 853 - 110 220
1940	110 221 - 110 614
1941	110 615 - 110 944
1942	110 945 - 111 218
1943	111 219 - 111 390
1944	111 391 - 111 928
1945	111 929 - 112 878
1946	112 879 - 114 143
1947	114 144 - 114 943
1948	114 944 - 115 373

Standard 80 (3-speed)
| 1937 | 803 929 - 803 990 |
| 1938 | 803 991 - 805 319 |

Standard 80 (4-speed)
1938	805 320 - 805 376
1939	805 377 - 806 879
1940	806 880 - 808 124
1941	808 125 - 809 050
1942	809 051 - 809 990
1943	809 991 - 810 469
1944	810 470 - 811 990
1945	811 991 - 813 066
1946	813 067 - 814 563
1947	814 564 - 815 215
1948	815 216 - 816 241

Models 90 & 99 (4-cylinder)

Year	Serial Numbers
1937	508 918 - 508 934
1938	508 935 - 509 611
1939	509 612 - 510 067
1940	510 068 - 510 563
1941	510 564 - 510 976
1942	510 977 - 511 295
1943	511 296 - 511 473
1944	511 474 - 512 043
1945	512 044 - 512 820
1946	512 821 - 513 105
1947	513 106 - 513 855
1948	513 856 - 514 855
1949	514 856 - 516 275
1950	516 276 - 516 887
1951	516 888 - 517 873
1952	517 874 - 518 212

Model HG Crawler

Year	Serial Numbers
1945	13GA422 - 19GA992
1946	19GA994 - 25GA238
1947	25GA240 - 33GA144
1948	33GA146 - 41GA894
1949	41GA896 - 48GA426
1950	48GA428 - 55GA429
1951	55GA430 - 59GA000

Model HGR Crawler

Year	Serial Numbers
1945	1NA000 - 1NA048
1946	None Built
1947	1NA050 - 1NA704
1948	1NA706

Row Crop 66

Year	Serial Numbers
1949	420 001 - 423 100
1950	423 101 - 426 010
1951	426 011 - 429 770
1952	429 771 - 431 472
1953	3 503 990 - 3 510 962*
1954	4 500 309 - 4 503 563*

Standard 66

Year	Serial Numbers
1949	470 001 - 471 050

Year	Serial Numbers
1950	471 051 - 472 390
1951	472 391 - 474 232
1952	474 233 - 476 408
1953	3 504 001 - 3 511 337*
1954	4 501 624 - 4 504 476*

Row Crop 77

Year	Serial Numbers
1948	320 001 - 320 240
1949	320 241 - 327 900
1950	327 901 - 337 242
1951	337 243 - 347 903
1952	347 904 - 354 447
1953	3 500 001 - 3 510 830*
1954	4 501 301 - 4 504 470*

Standard 77

Year	Serial Numbers
1948	269 001 - 269 940
1949	269 941 - 271 266
1950	271 267 - 272 465
1951	272 466 - 273 375
1952	273 376 - 274 051
1953	None Built
1954	None Built

Row Crop 88 (Streamline)

Year	Serial Numbers
1947	120 001 - 120 352
1948	120 353 - 121 300

Row Crop 88 (Fleetline)

Year	Serial Numbers
1948	121 301 - 123 300
1949	123 301 - 128 652
1950	128 653 - 132 862
1951	132 863 - 138 183
1952	138 184 - 143 232
1953	3 500 977 - 3 511 566*
1954	4 500 076 - 4 505 123*

Standard 88 (Streamline)

Year	Serial Numbers
1947	820 001 - 820 135
1948	820 136 - 820 485

Standard 88 (Fleetline)

Year	Serial Numbers
1948	820 486 - 821 085

Year	Serial Numbers
1949	821 086 - 824 240
1950	824 241 - 825 810
1951	825 811 - 826 916
1952	826 917 - 827 966
1953	3 501 813 - 3 511 484*
1954	4 500 080 - 4 505 081*

Model 99 (Styled & 6-cylinders)

Year	Serial Numbers
1952	518 300 - 518 313
1953	518 314 - 519 292

Model OC-3 Crawler

Year	Serial Numbers
1951	1WH000 - 3WH711
1952	3WH712 - 11WH759
1953	3 500 001 - and up
1954	4 500 005 - and up
1955	11WH760 - 155WH305
1956	15WH306 - 19WH089
1957	19WH090 - and up

Model OC-6 Crawler, Gasoline

Year	Serial Numbers
1953	3 502 785 - and up
1954	4 500 002 - and up
1955	1RM182 - 1RM313
1956	1RM314 - 1RM503
1957	1RM504 - 1RM807
1958	1RM808 - 2RM003
1959	2RM004 - 2RM125
1960	2RM126 - and up

Model OC-6 Crawler, Diesel

Year	Serial Numbers
1953	3 502 776 - and up
1954	4 500 007 - and up
1955	1RC468 - 1RC631
1956	1RC632 - 1RC875
1957	1RC876 - 2RC261
1958	2RC262 - 2RC365
1959	2RC366 - 2RC457
1960	2RC458 - and up

Super 44

Year	Serial Numbers
1957	1 001 - 1 550
1958	1 551 - 1 775

Super 55

Year	Serial Numbers
1954	6 001 - 8 290
1955	11 837 - 31 370
1956	35 001 - 43 647
1957	43 916 - 56 036
1958	56 501 - 59 033

Super 66

Year	Serial Numbers
1954	7 085 - 7 284
1955	14 099 - 27 842
1956	39 371 - 42 430
1957	45 846 - 55 800
1958	57 858 - 72 824

Super 77

Year	Serial Numbers
1954	8 303 - 8 988
1955	10 001 - 29 842
1956	38 500 - 43 637
1957	44 167 - 55 955
1958	56 917 - 59 008

Super 88

Year	Serial Numbers
1954	6 503 - 8 302
1955	10 075 - 29 347
1956	36 774 - 43 715
1957	43 901 - 55 607
1958	56 580 - 59 001

Super 99 & Super 99 GM

Year	Serial Numbers
1954	519 300 - 519 675
1955	519 676 - 520 455
1956	520 456 - 520 943
1957	520 944 - 521 612
1958	521 613 - 521 635

*Starting in 1953 one series of serial numbers was used for all models of wheel type tractors built at Charles City. Note the first two digits for 1953 and 1954 are the year in reverse order.

Model 440

1960	85 725 - 87 817
1962	121 833 - 122 542

Model 500

1960	100 001 - 100 500
1961	100 501 - 101 200
1962	101 201 - 101 700
1963	101 701 - 102 000

Model 550

1958	60 501 - 70 745
1959	72 632 - 84 415
1960	84 416 - 110 966
1961	111 868 - 117 540
1962	117 541 - 123 699
1963	127 365 - 140 619
1964	140 620 - 149 764
1965	162 265 - 163 114
1966	171 923 - 176 454
1967	186 165 - 193 085
1968	206 095 - 207 856
1969	213 340 - 217 921
1970	222 833 - 223 056
1971	226 965 - 227 120
1972	232 918 - 235 123
1973	238 237 - 242 700
1974	248 375 - 254 410
1975	259 255 - 259 491

Model 600

1962	449 800 - 452 300
1963	452 301 - 453 700

Model 660

1959	73 132 - 84 553
1960	86 166 - 110 955
1961	111 213 - 117 266
1962	117 873 - 126 294
1963	127 356 - 136 486
1964	141 160 - 144 039

Model 770

1958	60 504 - 70 891

1959	71 011 - 84 384
1960	84 554 - 110 967
1961	111 472 - 117 516
1962	117 600 - 126 208
1963	127 319 - 138 612
1964	141 901 - 149 064
1965	153 255 - 165 092
1966	171 515 - 178 936
1967	183 649 - 193 365

Model 880

1958	60 505 - 71 317
1959	71 640 - 84 335
1960	84 555 - 110 954
1961	111 262 - 117 504
1962	117 640 - 126 354
1963	128 911 - 135 054

Model 950, 990 GM, & 995 GM

1958	530 001 - 530 387
	67 828 - 71 112
1959	71 245 - 84 376
1960	84 487 - 95 350
1961	110 064 - 115 469

Model 1600

1962	124 420 - 127 043
1963	127 044 - 140 262
1964	140 723 - 147 568

Model 1800, A, B, & C

1960 (A)	90 525 - 111 024
1961 (A)	111 025 - 117 375
1962 (A)	118 344 - 124 395
1962 (B)	124 397 - 126 352
1963 (B)	129 286 - 134 683
1963 (C)	136 501 - 140 085
1964 (C)	140 893 - 149 818

Model 1900, A, B, & C

1960 (A)	90 532 - 111 022
1961 (A)	111 028 - 117 374
1962 (A)	118 356 - 124 372
1962 (B)	124 396 - 126 355

1963 (B)	128 422 - 135 430
1963 (C)	138 440 - 140 066
1964 (C)	141 168 - 148 651

Model 1250

1965	705 376 - 712 832
1966	712 833 - 725 780
1967	728 661 - 739 518
1968	739 527 - 742 520
1969	742 526 - 743 152

Model 1450

1967	132 382 - 147 473
1968	147 482 - 155 196
1969	155 479 - 159 945

Model 1550

1965	157 841 - 166 406
1966	168 919 - 181 061
1967	184 488 - 196 205
1968	196 301 - 208 959
1969	213 243 - 218 186

Model 1650

1964	149 836 - 152 569
1965	153 855 - 167 667
1966	167 668 - 183 194
1967	183 923 - 195 765
1968	201 091 - 209 251
1969	212 733 - 218 193

Model 1750

1966	181 062 - 182 126
1967	185 301 - 200 216
1968	200 217 - 211 777
1969	214 936 - 218 850

Model 1850

1964	150 421 - 153 013
1965	153 014 - 167 285
1966	168 127 - 183 381
1967	183 382 - 199 964
1968	200 360 - 212 448
1969	212 673 - 218 852

Model 1950

1964	150 492 - 153 011
1965	153 016 - 167 298
1966	168 190 - 177 661
1967	189 008 - 199 186

Model 1950-T

1967	188 974 - 199 339
1968	201 931 - 211 117
1969	213 376 - 218 449

Model 2050

1968	204 444 - 212 527
1969	212 560 - 213 932

Model 2150

1968	204 480 - 212 553
1969	212 554 - 216 595

Models 1250A & 1255

1969 (1250A)	305 985 - 309 380
1969 (1255)	309 381 - 360 743
1970 (1255)	312 957 - 318 393
1971 (1255)	317 338 - 318 385

Model 1265

1971	302 402 - 303 466
1972	304 497 - 307 220
1973	307 221 - 314 368
1974	314 369 - 319 893
1975	317 000 - 321 497

Model 1355

1969	503 287 - 512 149
1970	512 698 - 525 078
1971	523 254 - 526 640

Model 1365

1971	706 251 - 712 386
1972	706 277 - 716 975
1973	714 614 - 730 076
1974	725 451 - 764 138
1975	729 125 - 766 614

Model 1465

1973	827 183 - 831 562
1974	827 580 - 839 423
1975	827 287 - 839 487

Model 1555

1969	218 128 - 220 639
1970	221 295 - 223 072
1971	225 914 - 230 893
1972	232 089 - 235 984
1973	236 883 - 242 906
1974	244 937 - 250 430
1975	256 165 - 262 877

Model 1655

1969	218 025 - 220 399
1970	222 600 - 222 761
1971	225 997 - 230 735
1972	231 772 - 235 188
1973	236 586 - 244 447
1974	244 735 - 255 515
1975	257 700 - 263 340

Model 1755

1970	221 603 - 223 322
1971	226 445 - 229 636
1972	231 415 - 236 163
1973	238 136 - 244 369
1974	245 667 - 253 668
1975	257 515 - 260 346

Model 1855

1969	220 640 - 221 098
1970	221 099 - 223 507
1971	225 508 - 231 365
1972	231 366 - 236 584
1973	236 585 - 244 489
1974	247 436 - 254 772
1975	255 727 - 255 785

Model 1865 (MM G950)

1971	43 600 416 - 43 600 829

Model 1955

1970	222 304 - 223 439
1971	226 858 - 230 456
1972	232 958 - 236 326
1973	239 032 - 244 558
1974	247 871 - 253 050

Model 2055 (MM G1050)

1971	43 100 416 - 43 100 544

Model 2155 (MM G1350)

1971	43 300 043 - 43 300 253

Model 2255

1972	235 598 - 235 999
1973	237 210 - 244 214
1974	244 825 - 252 714
1975	258 472 - 258 571
1976	266 683 - 266 782

Model 2455 (MM A4T-1400)

1969	43 900 001 - 43 900 102
1970	43 900 103 - 43 900 247

Model 2655 (MM A4T-1600)

1971	45 600 188 - 45 600 700
1972	45 600 701 - 45 601 190

White Field Boss

Model 2-50

1976 (2wd)	516 625 - 518 781
1976 (fwd)	516 898 - 518 993
1977 (2wd)	518 782 - 520 783
1977 (fwd)	518 994 - 521 634
1978 (2wd)	520 784 - 525 267
1978 (fwd)	521 635 - 525 289
1979 (2wd)	525 268 - 525 725
1979 (fwd)	525 290 - 527 580
1980 (2wd)	525 726 - 527 626
1980 (fwd)	527 581 - 527 687

Model 2-60

1976 (2wd)	780 725 - 790 272

1976 (fwd)	782 037 - 790 272
1977 (2wd)	790 273 - 944 701
1977 (fwd)	790 273 - 946 284
1978 (2wd)	944 702 - 959 279
1978 (fwd)	946 285 - 959 302
1979 (2wd)	959 280 - 959 999
	480 187 - 491 334
1979 (fwd)	959 303 - 959 999
	480 307 - 486 531

Model 2-70

1976	266 173 - 273 088
1977	274 543 - 281 876
1978	283 917 - 284 276
1979	287 528 - 292 563
1980	293 819 - 294 062
1981	296 246 - 298 946
1982	299 887 - 300 091

Model 2-85

1975	263 341 - 265 402
1976	268 142 - 273 315
1977	274 287 - 281 504
1978	282 339 - 287 196
1979	287 469 - 293 408
1980	294 063 - 295 791
1981	297 751 - 299 123
1982	300 092 - 300 158

Model 2-105

1974	255 216 - 255 537
1975	255 538 - 265 927
1976	265 928 - 273 619
1977	273 760 - 280 588
1978	282 102 - 287 189
1979	287 197 - 293 357
1980	294 109 - 295 781
1981	296 878 - 299 731
1982	300 779 - 300 782

Model 2-135

1976	272 663 - 273 628
1977	273 629 - 282 078
1978	282 825 - 286 928

1979	288 201 - 293 818
1980	294 330 - 296 128
1981	296 611 - 299 632
1982	300 380 - 300 693

Model 2-150

1975	257 899 - 265 201
1976	266 783 - 271 312

Model 2-155

1976	272 595 - 272 812
1977	276 055 - 281 209
1978	282 280 - 286 929
1979	287 812 - 293 708
1980	296 160 - 296 244
1981	297 134 - 299 365
1982	300 259 - 300 429

Model 2-180

1977	281 993 - 282 087
1978	282 088 - 286 004
1979	289 447 - 292 891
1980	294 655 - 294 821
1981	296 571 - 299 002
1982	300 159 - 300 258

Model 4-150

1974	246 001 - 246 849
1975	246 871 - 262 243
1976	262 244 - 267 958
1977	275 051 - 275 405
1978	275 406 - 275 571

Model 4-175

1979	292 187 - 292 334
1980	295 808 - 295 900
1981	297 293 - 299 848
1982	299 849 - 299 886

Model 4-180

1975	256 587 - 262 099
1976	262 524 - 268 111
1977	268 112 - 275 396
1978	275 450 - 275 502

Model 4-210

1978	275 572 - 275 943
1979	275 944 - 292 368
1980	295 391 - 296 205
1981	296 471 - 299 826
1982	300 694 - 300 778

Model 2-30

1979-84   001 418 - 101 461

Model 2-32

1985-86   000 007 - 000 315

Model 2-35

1979-84   005 822 - 004 001

Model 2-45

1979-81   000 001 - 000 548

Model 2-55

1982-87   000 097 - 000 807

Model 2-62

1979-81   000 001 - 001 143

Model 2-65

1982-87   000 099 - 001 202

Model 2-75

1982-87   000 177 - 000 955

Model 2-88

1982	301 457 - 301 717
1983	None Built
1984	302 464 - 302 599
1985	None Built
1986	400 001 - 400 599
1987	400 734 - 400 762

Model 2-110

1982	300 783 - 301 965
1983	301 998 - 302 158

1984	302 334 - 303 551
1985	303 552 - 303 614
1986	400 231 - 400 609
1987	400 764 - 401 005

Model 2-135 Series 3

1982	301 116 - 301 811
1983	302 159 - 302 233
1984	302 715 - 303 289
1985	None Built
1986	400 167 - 400 733
1987	400 831 - 400 880

Model 2-155 Series 3

1982	300 928 - 301 921
1983	None Built
1984	302 791 - 303 344
1985	None Built
1986	400 107 - 400 718

Model 2-180 Series 3

1982	301 922 - 310 963
1983	301 966 - 301 997
1984	302 951 - 302 990
1985	None Built
1986	400 082 - 400 230

Model 4-225

1983	302 234 - 302 273
1984	302 620 - 303 468
1985	None Built
1986	400 344
1987	400 901 - 400 921

Model 4-270

1983	302 274 - 302 333
1984	302 655 - 303 423
1985	None Built
1986	400 639 - 400 658
1987	400 922 - 400 941
1988	401 411 - 401 435

White

Model FB 16

1986-89 (2wd) 02 314 - 02 811
1986-89 (fwd) 14 422 - 16 865

Model FB 21

1986-89 (2wd) 00 595 - 01 181
1986-89 (fwd) 02 879 - 04 844

Model FB 31

1986-89 (2wd) 00 126 - 01 981
1986-89 (fwd) 00 028 - 01 061

Model FB 37

1986-89 (2wd) 00 083 - 00 315
1986-89 (fwd) 00 679 - 01 339

Model FB 43

1986-89 (2wd) 00 060 - 00 156
1986-89 (fwd) 00 322 - 00 499

American 60

1989	402 965 - 403 164
1990	404 299 - 404 454
1991	405 028 - 405 047

American 80

1989	402 590 - 403 464
1990	404 266 - 404 541
1991	405 048 - 405 052

Model 100

1987	401 236 - 401 260
1988	401 361 - 401 970

Last Charles City 100 and the last Charles City tractor was 401 505

1989	402 661 - 403 764

Model 120

1987	401 121 - 401 235
1988	401 296 - 402 520

Last Charles City 120 was 401 485

1989	402 521 - 403 839

Model 125

1990	404 066 - 404 165
1991	404 601 - 404 969

Model 140

1987	401 151 - 401 200
1988	401 326 - 402 440

Last Charles City 140 was 401 360

1989	402 736 - 404 064

Model 145

1991	404 671 - 404 923

Model 160

1987	401 096 - 401 120
1988	401 261 - 402 220

Last Charles City 160 was 401 295

1989	403 640 - 404 024

Model 170

1990	404 228 - 404 265
1991	404 766 - 405 207

Model 185

1986 (FB 185) 400 659 - 400 708

1987	400 881 - 401 095

Last Charles City 185 was 401 095

1988	401 579 - 402 050
1989	402 761 - 404 014

Model 195

1990	404 166 - 404 227
1991	404 826 - 404 995

Additional Reading
Available from ASAE

A Tractor Goes Farming. Roy Harrington.

The Agricultural Tractor: 1855-1950. R.B. Gray.

Allis-Chalmers Farm Equipment 1914-1985. Norm Swinford.

A Guide to Allis-Chalmers Farm Tractors. Norm Swinford.

Classic Tractor Collectors: Restoring and Preserving Farm Power from the Past. John Harvey.

Farm Tractors: 1950-1975. Lester Larson.

Farm Tractors: 1975-1995. Larry Gay.

Full Steam Ahead: J.I. Case Tractors and Equipment 1842-1955. David Erb and Eldon Brumbaugh.

Hart-Parr Traction Engine Catalog.

How to Restore Your Farm Tractor. Robert Pripps.

How to Restore Tractor Magnetos. Neil Yerigan.

International Harvester Farm Equipment, Product History 1831-1985. Ralph Baumheckel and Kent Borghoff.

JI Case Agricultural & Construction Equipment 1956-1994, Vol. 2. Tom Stonehouse and Eldon Brumbaugh.

John Deere Buggies and Wagons. Ralph Hughes.

John Deere Tractors and Equipment, Vol. 1 and Vol. 2. Don Macmillan, Russell Jones, and Roy Harrington.

John Deere Tractors Worldwide: A Century of Progress, 1893-1993. Don Macmillan.

Books can be ordered from the American Society of Agricultural Engineers (ASAE), 2950 Niles Road, St. Joseph, Michigan 49085-9659, USA
Voice: (800) 695-2723 or (616) 428-6324; FAX: (616) 429-3852.

If you wish to be kept current on tractor equipment history publications, just ask for a free copy of the *Looking Back* catalog.

For information about the Hart-Parr/Oliver Collector's Association contact:
Hart-Parr/Oliver Collector's Association
Box 685
Charles City, IA 50616